Refreshing

Worship

For Mum and Dad,
and all at *Live on Planet Earth*,
who have dared to dream

Brian & Kevin Draper

Text copyright © Brian Draper and Kevin Draper 2000
The authors assert the moral right
to be identified as the authors of this work

Published by
The Bible Reading Fellowship
Peter's Way
Sandy Lane West
Oxford OX4 6HG
ISBN 1 84101 146 0

First published 2000
10 9 8 7 6 5 4 3 2 1 0

Acknowledgments
Unless otherwise stated, scripture quotations are taken from the *Holy Bible, New
International Version*, copyright © 1973, 1978, 1984 by International Bible Society,
used by permission of Hodder & Stoughton Limited. All rights reserved. 'NIV' is a
registered trademark of International Bible Society. UK trademark number 1448790.

A catalogue record for this book is available from the British Library

Printed and bound in Great Britain by Omnia Books Limited, Glasgow

CONTENTS

Setting out

Today we are on a journey: a journey towards the light that is God.
And out again.
A journey of receiving… and then giving.
Walk with expectancy!
As you journey, reflect on what you think. Expect to discover the
wonderful, the fantastic. Open your eyes wide, use your senses—this is
no senseless journey.

Breathe deeply. Relax. Don't rush. Savour the moment, as if it were
your last.
Or, perhaps, your first.
Be aware of others—we are wondering together. And focus on moving
Godwards.

As you move towards God, confess and let go of things that hinder
your relationship with him.

Shed images or projections of yourself so that you can be real with God.
Let go of what other people think you should be, their expectations of
you, their projections.

As you journey, unmask yourself; grow by subtraction. Prepare to meet
with God.

At the beginning of time the earth was in darkness; and we are in
darkness.
But we shall move towards the warmth and nourishment that is God,
our life source.

God spoke the word, and the Word was God.
And there was light.

God created and created and keeps on creating.
He sees that it is good.
She labours to bring life; and gives birth to abundance.
It is good.

Our task is seldom easy; after all, we see through a glass dimly.
But we have seen—maybe just glimpsed—the light, and we travel
as a symbol that we are going after the light of God.

As a seed grows towards the light, allow yourself to do the same.
Trust the Creator God with your whole self.
Acknowledge who you are, and who you are becoming.
Show your amazing colours. Stand tall.

Have you stopped to see how far you have come, recently?
Have you encouraged each other to press on?
As you journey, resolve to encourage those you travel with in faith
and life.

And remember the beautiful, strange paradox of our faith.
We search after God, we travel towards him, as a pilgrim.
And yet he, too, is with us. As a guide. And as a traveller.
He hasn't promised an easy ride. But he has promised to sustain us.

God is love. They will comfort you.
Three in One,
One, but not the same…
…as we are one, but not the same.
Connected, but individual.
Apart, but together.
A part of each other.

So reads the introduction to the Labyrinth, a form of contemporary 'service' that a few of us put together towards the end of our time as the alternative worship community *Live On Planet Earth* (*LOPE*). It had been a time of struggle, a time of joy, a time of knocking down and rebuilding. A handful of us from local churches in rural Kent had got together to see if we could 'do' church in a different way among ourselves, to make more sense of our own lives and cultures, and to reflect a theology which embraced not only our joy at being Christians—the sense that we had set out on a wonderful journey—but also the fact that we were still travelling. In the words of the famous U2 song, we still hadn't found what we were looking for, and we wanted to reflect this in our worship lives together. We had no idea of where it would lead, nor what the end product would look like.

That 'end product', in retrospect, was twofold. First, and by far the most important, was a loose-knit community of Christians and spiritual searchers who gathered once a month for a main service, and once a week (for those who wanted to) in small groups. The monthly service became, in some senses, the shop window; whereas the weekly meetings helped form the 'community'. There were those who had been battered and bruised by the Church, for whom alternative worship was to become something of a symbol of passive resistance to the abuses of Christian extremism; there were those who were simply disaffected with the mainstream Church, desiring something more awe-inspiring, more sensual, more spiritual; there were those who had never experienced church before, but had been brought along or who had simply walked in off the street; and there were those who came along to police us, to make sure we didn't stray off the straight and narrow and wander into the dangerous side-streets of spirituality (and who sometimes found that, in fact, it was *worth* coming off the concrete motorways and enjoying the scenic route for a change). Young and old alike—this was never a 'mission' to youth as such, and neither is most alternative worship—became empowered to think about their faith in new, creative ways. We learned, in effect, not to do church, but to 'be' a kind of community.

Second, the end product was the practical outworking of doing worship differently—creatively. We started by trying to jazz up choruses, not really knowing where it would take us. We ended with a service called 'the Labyrinth' that we took on the road to numerous venues from dusty church halls to national conferences and festivals such as Brainstormers and Greenbelt. Earlier this year, a collaboration between LOPE, *Grace* and *Epicentre* put on a version of the Labyrinth at St Paul's Cathedral in London. Our version of the Labyrinth has been 'walked' by thousands of people from tourists to vicars and pilgrims to youth workers— mostly enthusiastic, normal Christians who realized they could worship God in a different way, by plundering ancient and modern traditions alike and finding the experience more real and more deeply related to the issues that face them in a world of pluralism, relativism and consumerism.

The Labyrinth

To start at the end of our journey, the Labyrinth is a walking meditation, based on an ancient form of pre-Christian ritual which was later adopted by Christians in their own worship. The earliest remaining example can be seen, and walked, on the floor of Chartres Cathedral in France. It looks like a maze, but in fact it is a circular path that leads you on an 'inward journey' towards a central space, then out again. You can't go wrong; there are no choices to be made about which way you go. Labyrinths come in all sorts of shapes and sizes, and their paths have been hewn in stone or marked out by string or carved by a stick in the sand. It is a simple, spiritual exercise; alternative worship communities, in rediscovering the Labyrinth, have found that it is a contemplative, spiritual aid to worship at a time when life seems to get busier and shallower by the day.

The Labyrinth symbolizes our walk with God. You walk it slowly, and take at least half an hour to complete it. In the version we designed, as you walk you are encouraged at various points to stop and think about a range of things: faith as a journey; your fellow travelling companions; the symbolism of light and dark; your identity as a human being in relation to yourself, each other, the creation and God; the forces of contemporary culture and consumerism; the ecological issues facing the planet today; issues of forgiving and of being forgiven...

Ours is usually set in a darkened room, with ambient music playing,[1] and voiceovers and visuals (on TVs and screens and banners). It is primarily a relaxed, spiritual space in which to spend an hour or two sitting, kneeling, lying, praying, thinking, worshipping. Not everyone can go through the Labyrinth at once, so in our version we have three 'stations' outside of the path where people can model clay, construct prayer trees, paint, write or plant seeds. These stations allow people to explore specifically their relationships to others, themselves and the planet. Within the Labyrinth itself, which serves as the 'relating to God' station, we use nightlights (small candles) to help symbolize our own faith and experience of God, as we prepare to come before him (with our lights unlit). God is symbolized as a larger candle in the central space. Once we have taken time to pray and think and experience his love, we then light our own candles, and take them, symbolically again, on the 'outward journey' into the world—drawing on John's prologue that says that 'the true light that gives light to every person was coming into the world' (John 1:9). The outward journey in particular emphasizes the theological and practical theme of incarnation, which is so beautifully rendered in John's prologue. It is a recurring motif for us and for most alternative worshippers.

We created our own design for the Labyrinth (the 'original' at Chartres is complex and needs lots of space). Many 'alternative' worshippers have also designed their own, and found it helpful as they contemplate their own corporate and individual spiritual journeys. You can, of course, do the same. We shall refer to the Labyrinth at times throughout the book, as for us it not only symbolizes our walk with God, but it helps crystallize many of the key themes that developed in our thinking and being as a community of alternative worshippers, as we sought to relate our faith to life in the twenty-first century. We hope that you will find it useful—and perhaps inspirational.

We shall also refer to our services at *Live On Planet Earth*. This isn't because we feel they were the best you could ever get (although some of the times we had worshipping there *were* the most authentic and inspiring times of worship that *we* had enjoyed). But we use the example because it is what we know and have experienced. There are many other wonderful examples across the country of creative and alternative worship groups in action—all with their own stories, their own struggles, their own disasters and their own triumphs. Maybe there is one near you: have a look on Greenbelt's website (see the Appendix of Resources). Our experience is of *Live On Planet Earth*, and a similar service, *Grace*, in north-west London; and that is what we shall refer to. This is a part of our story.

We started, as we said, by meeting to ask how we could recontextualize our worship[2] to enable the experience to be more authentic to our own lives and cultures. What began as something that resembled a youth service developed, over five long and hard years (at many times we faced opposition from traditionalists and wanted to give up), into something that looked and felt very different. Our original inspiration had come from the Nine O'Clock Service in Sheffield. This service tragically collapsed and its demise—through one man, Chris Brain—has been widely documented.[3] But the Nine O'Clock Service in fact was a source of inspiration for many new services—the theological path they were forging was, to all intents and purposes, both exciting and innovative. It was what Brain ended up *doing*—not what he was saying—that caused the service to disintegrate. It is important to separate these two things, because otherwise anything 'alternative' will be tarred with the same brush, and rejected without being given a chance to flourish. In fact, the allegation that we would become 'another NOS' was thrown at us regularly by those who were opposed to what we were doing; but we put in place the kind of accountability structures which embraced safe practice procedures (something important for all churches to be aware of). 'Abuse' takes place in many situations, whether it be in the family, in schools, in mainstream churches or wherever. It is not enough to equate alternative worship with abuse simply because of the misdemeanours of one man.

There are many alternative services that are alive and well: *The Late Late Service* in Glasgow, for example, for us became a more accessible (and achievable) example of a radical worship community that really seemed to work, and to reflect the concerns of many creative and socially aware Christians who felt that church wasn't all that it was cracked up to be. At the heart of alternative worship, and at the heart of what we saw and experienced through *The Late Late Service* and other groups (crucially given space at events such as Greenbelt in the late 1980s), there was a desire for healing, for holism, for depth, for spiritual and biblical engagement—which gave us hope that, somehow, worship could be different. It didn't have to be *either* dry, stale hymns (which seemed to symbolize all that was dead about the Church) *or* charismatic choruses which claimed 'victory' and represented the triumphal and at times imperialist nature of the Church in the West. It could look and feel more like our own culture outside the Church. For many city-based alternative worship groups, there was more of a 'nightclub' feel to their projects, which drew mainly from the dance culture within which they felt at home. For *Live On Planet Earth*, in rural Kent, we reflected the influences that arose from a variety of social and cultural settings, ranging from deprived village estates to well-heeled grammar schools. The lesson we began to learn was that worship should reflect the concerns and culture of our local community.

At this point, it is very important to lay down your misconceptions about 'alternative' worship before reading on. The press typically describes such services as 'rave in the nave'— yet many services are, in fact, nothing like that. Many are quiet and contemplative. Most alternative worship in fact prides itself on drawing from a range of musical genres and traditions, not just dance music. Whenever we speak at conferences or seminars about alternative worship, we come across people who would love to try something different, but who think that unless they have a huge budget and/or lots of hi-tech equipment and technicians, they won't be able to. The reality couldn't be more different; indeed, it is actually far better to start low-tech and on a shoe-string. You will be more likely to think creatively and less likely to make the mistake of letting the gadgets dictate the content of the service. The other misconception is that alternative worship equates to liberalism. While many groups have explored beyond the confines of traditional evangelicalism and have tried to allow their theology to develop and grow, this takes place firmly within the Christian tradition.

So, to set the scene. At a typical service at *LOPE*, you would walk into the old congregational church in Cranbrook High Street, through a sheet of muslin that was glowing in ultraviolet light and that had our logo projected on to it. Inside, there were no chairs or pews (these had been removed in the hours leading up to the service by a hardworking and dedicated crew!), only cushions on the floor. High in the vaults of the building were more sheets, on which huge images would be projected. TVs and video screens were spread around the floor, so that most people could get a decent view of the visuals. Banners were draped all around the edge of the darkened worship area. There would probably be some quiet, ambient music being played as people waited for the service to begin.

Our desire throughout was to work alongside mainstream churches (indeed our work arose from an inter-denominational youthwork project)—not as an evangelistic 'bridge' with which to carry non-believers off the streets and into their own congregations. Rather, it was to let those who would otherwise be drifting away from church altogether find the kind of space they wouldn't normally get at church to continue to worship, to explore, sometimes to doubt, but to search after God within an authentic Christian spirituality. Our relationship with local churches was both painful and positive. We were sometimes a thorn in their side, and sometimes a creative example to them of how they might incorporate a greater degree of creativity within their own services. The debate would rage as to whether we were a church in our own right (something we never claimed for ourselves, as we didn't want to set up another institution) or a monthly evangelistic event. In the end, we were something in between—a collection of people who could come and go, who didn't have to sign on the dotted line, yet who began to feel genuinely that they belonged to each other.

Our own examples, and those you may already have experienced at other services, serve simply as encouragement. In the five years that we journeyed together as Live On Planet Earth, we saw people coming to faith, coming back to faith, hanging on by their fingernails to faith, and of course, sometimes dropping away. Yet we all, at times, discovered a spiritual depth in following Jesus that, for whatever reason, seemed to be lacking from all the various churches in our locality. We don't believe that this was unique to rural Kent; the same thing has been happening across the country, and across the world.

The motivations were therefore both cultural and theological. And, as we seek to explain through a variety of examples within this book, they were manifested in simple, practical and usually low-tech methods. We hope that the blend of all three—the cultural, theological and practical—will at least help you to understand a little more of what this journey was all about.

We say 'was', because we dismantled *Live On Planet Earth* in 1997, at a time when people were moving on and away. It was never meant to become another institution: we held lightly to our methods and to the service as a whole, because we recognize that we move on, spiritually and geographically. We have continued to take the Labyrinth to those who might otherwise never experience alternative worship. We have been involved with mainstream churches. And we have continued with forms of alterative worship. But along the way, we have tried to grow and learn from the mistakes that we made and the successes that we witnessed— and to be creative in how we worship, as we continue to struggle to integrate our faith with our lives, inside and outside the Church. It continues to be a wonderful journey. We hope that for a short while you will journey with us, and gain something from the experience of some very human, and very humble, attempts to dream a dream of faith.

ONE

Alternative what?

Alternative worship services raise a number of significant questions, such as 'Why are congregations like *Grace* and *Live On Planet Earth* "doing church" so differently?' It's our belief that the differences reflect not merely cosmetic changes to the style of church services, but rather a significant theological rethink too. One thing is clear: if the Church does not perceive the need for an ongoing renewal of its theology (and how it interacts with our contemporary lives) then we shall not look for new ways of worshipping.

In reading this book, perhaps you are looking primarily for ideas that can be taken from alternative worship services and recycled in your own situation. And while it may help in that way, we hope to encourage you to dig beneath the surface and discover the traditions, the thinking and the biblical themes which have motivated our quest. In so doing, you will gain an enhanced ability to engage effectively with the needs of both your existing congregation and those people you want to reach out to. Our aim is to provoke a pattern of reflection and thinking in your approach to Christian worship that will provide you with an almost limitless supply of practical ideas for the ongoing process of revitalizing corporate worship.

To talk about the need for an 'alternative' may suggest that things aren't perfect and that there is a problem with the existing expressions of worship within the Church in the United Kingdom. Although it could be argued that, in recent years, many people have resumed a 'search for spirituality', the Church *is* in fact in decline. (The most recent survey suggests that both the Church of England and the Roman Catholic Church have seen Sunday attendance drop by between 40 and 50 per cent over the last two decades.)[4] Of course, we can point to individual congregations (or even denominations) for examples of growth, but the statistics show that as we ended the 'decade of evangelism', people were still flooding out, not flocking back to church. As the leading sociologist of religion, Malcom Hamilton, points out, 'Secularization has greatly undermined the traditional churches, but it has not produced an irreligious population, only an unchurched one. Even in areas of low church membership, belief in the supernatural remains high.'[5] People are turning increasingly to other forms of spirituality (such as the range of alternatives offered by the New Age), and this in itself stands as an indictment of the failure of mainstream Christianity to connect with many searchers, both in terms of mission and worship.

We cannot lay the problem solely at the door of the evangelists. In today's context, where much weight is given to experience, the style of our services may have more to do with the *relative appeal* of Christianity than the rational presentation of the gospel message. It has been said that people are more likely to ask, 'Does it work?' rather than 'Is it true?' The way we worship—the language, imagery, metaphors, music and even the layout and design of our buildings and 'worship spaces'—says a lot to people outside the church about our God. Is our God easily definable, or mysterious? Passionate or listless? Loving or vengeful? Active or impassive? Remote or involved? Creative or restrictive? The elements that comprise our acts of worship speak volumes about our theology, so it is crucial that we take time to evaluate them.

Cultural considerations

Many people believe that the Western world is undergoing a huge shift from the modern era to something postmodern. To say that the term 'postmodern' has become a cliché is something of an understatement, and the whole area is fraught with scholarly disagreements. The point is that, however one interprets the changes, we are in the midst of the largest shift in the way we in the 'West' view the world for some 200 or so years. It's not only a time of unrivalled change, but of great opportunity for religion, which has now been set free from the hold of reason and rationality.

While we may not be convinced by, or even aware of, the theories of postmodernism, we are all, to a greater or lesser degree, affected by the cultural impact of postmodernity. Few people don't own televisions, for instance, and aren't bombarded with a never-ending stream of images. We are all, to a greater or lesser extent, part of the change from a word-based culture to an image-based culture. We are all affected by the market forces of consumer culture, and by the unparalleled technological change which affects the way we live, work and spend our leisure time. Those are the cultural manifestations of postmodernity. The philosophical manifestations may, we like to think, have made less of a dent on us as Christians: we believe still in truth, whereas postmodern philosophers do not. But this does not mean we should not engage critically with them, as, for starters, their theories have filtered down to the wider population, and can be seen clearly in action through pluralism and relativism. They do, indeed, affect the person on the street. By and large, alternative worship groups have encompassed those who feel more comfortable within the changing culture. Their particularities can offer insights to a church that is now dealing with people who are affected, for good or bad, by a multitude of new cultures.

The convergence of the emerging postmodern era with the dawn of a new millennium presents a unique opportunity to the Church to re-evaluate the way it enables people to worship. The time is ripe to explore new ways of worshipping God—ways rooted in biblical orthodoxy and the full range of Christian tradition, but at the same time reflecting, engaging with, and emerging from the particular needs of today.

The vital question is, how are we to interact with the people of this postmodern world and at the same time maintain our integrity and distinctiveness? How can we engage with the changing concerns and emphases of the postmodern world, the spirit of the age, without capitulating to it? Andrew Walker has commented: 'There will be no place for the broad church in the postmodern world. The future will lie in communities, sects and the monastery.'[6] The phrase 'In the world but not of it' is a well-worn cliché, yet it remains true, and something that we strive to work out in real-life situations. This is an issue that is integral not only to worship but to all areas of corporate and individual Christian life and witness.

In recent years, the metaphor of pilgrimage has come to serve as a timely reminder and a 'control' to another metaphor—that of the 'two kingdoms'. The Church has, up to now, emphasized that you are either 'in' or 'out' of the Kingdom of God, often on the basis of affiliation to church (and in some more arrogant cases, to a particular denomination). In rediscovering the idea of pilgrimage—of being on a spiritual journey (whether we see that as pressing onwards towards the goal, running the race, taking up our cross to follow Jesus, or whatever)—we owe much to the postmodern emphasis on *process*. So, we can view salvation as more of a process than a one-off event in our lives.

This means simply acknowledging the reality that, for most people, becoming a Christian is a process which is occasionally punctuated by moments of crisis. Such observations affect not only the shape of our approach to mission but also our worship. This is no aimless or meaningless wandering that we are on: we have a goal, of a restored relationship with God. Many of us can look back on moments in our lives, even before we may have called ourselves 'Christian', when we were being drawn Godwards by the Holy Spirit. We were already on a pilgrimage towards God. Often such moments occur in the context of Christian worship.

Similarly, many people brought up in 'Christian homes' may remember years and years of Sunday schools and youth groups before they made any kind of explicit 'commitment to Christ'. One Baptist minister we knew when we were young could not remember the exact day he became a Christian. His embarrassment was such that he invented a date which he used if and when he was quizzed. His experience of becoming a Christian was one of a gradually deepening relationship with Christ that began in his life as early as he could remember. This is something that many Christians can, and should happily, identify with.

If a church's theology and understanding of salvation revolve equally or even predominantly around this 'journey' metaphor, then both the content and style of its worship should naturally reflect this. It will probably be more inclined to ensure that its services are accessible and inclusive for the whole community, not just focused on the select few who have 'seen the film, got the badge and wear the T-shirt'. For many alternative worship groups, the 'labyrinth' has become an enduring symbol and an integral part of their worship. We shall elaborate more on this later; suffice to say that it has been wonderfully liberating to use such an evocative element of our Christian heritage to reflect our ongoing need to journey towards God, and to integrate this journey with our whole lives and our relationship with others. So our acts of worship and our theology inevitably feed off one another. Many alternative worship groups naturally reflect their theological emphasis on spiritual pilgrimage.

Honest, authentic, whole-life worship

The service at *Live On Planet Earth* arose initially from our desire to enable young people—as well as ourselves—to worship God in a way that reflected their true identities. In other words, we wanted to help them find an authentic way of worshipping that allowed them to be honest in their relationship with God. Our

work was influenced by Pete Ward's Oxford Youth Works project
—which focuses on relationship—and by a book by the
theologian Colin Gunton, *The One, the Three and the Many*,[7] which
discusses the need for humans to enjoy healthy relationships with
God, other people, the rest of 'creation' and themselves. We were
inspired by Gunton's desire to reinstate an understanding of God
as trinitarian community.

Our work with young people in Kent was driven by the desire
to enable them to find reconciliation and wholeness in each of the
four areas highlighted by Gunton. We strove for authenticity. So it
was essential that what they did at church, in worshipping the
God with whom they were seeking a reconciled relationship,
reflected who they really were. Additionally, as we were seeking an
authenticity and a wholeness in our own lives, we became aware
of the need to subject our familiar expressions of worship to an
honest critique. We sought to shape an integrated spirituality that
reflected the reality of our ongoing pilgrimage and journey as
Christians in rural Kent in the late twentieth century. *Live On
Planet Earth* became a gathering point for a culturally and
demographically diverse group of people wanting to be part of a
creative collaboration of authentic worship.

We can't stress enough that this book raises issues of
importance to people regardless of age and cultural taste—they
do not just affect 'youth'. They are seen more explicitly in the
context of youth work, hence the tendency for youth work to
embrace the trappings. But it soon became clear to us that this
was not solely or even particularly a 'youth' issue. In fact, most
'alternative' worship groups are not primarily comprised of young
people. If you are prepared to critique your own patterns of
worship, or encourage others to do so, you will be opening a
Pandora's box of issues that may previously have lain dormant.
Do not embark on this journey lightly. Yet, with courage and
resolve, you can take the first teetering steps towards revitalizing
your worship, and making it accessible to people outside the

influence of your church, as well as the malcontents within.

How does this differ from any other church's ambitions and motivations? At *Live On Planet Earth* we had no real blueprint, and ended up with something that was vastly different from that which we had experienced in church before. As we began to reflect on our journey and how the service had come to be, we realized that it was not just different in terms of style—in fact, we ended up with some fundamentally different characteristics from the 'norm'.

Toolbox, not flatpack

You can use this book to equip you with the skills and tools that can be used, in the power of the Holy Spirit, to shape an authentic expression of worship for your particular situation. Although each of the areas highlighted in the subsequent chapters is important, they do not fit together like an IKEA flatpack. You can't build an identical model by following the instruction manual. The application of creative or alternative worship will result in very different expressions depending on the particular context. We do not want to provide you with pre-packaged answers but to provoke and encourage you to ask the right questions of your own tradition that will enable it to thrive.

This book can be used as a resource in one of two ways: either as a guide to revamping the forms and expressions of worship in existing services, and/or as a resource to enable you to start an additional service to complement those offered by your church. 'Alternative worship' need not be a source of controversy within your own church, if you allow space—at whatever point is suitable for you and your congregation, even 'on the edges'—for a degree of experimentation. In fact, we believe that in terms of mission, it is vital for leaders to ask proactively, 'How can our worship apply to the groups and cultures that are not represented among us but who live in the local community?'

Positive critique, not negative criticism

So, the themes of alternative worship outlined in this book primarily act as a critique of our patterns of worship, allowing us to reflect on how captivating and authentic our acts of worship are, and how they reflect our relationship with God—and by facilitating this for others, especially those who remain on the periphery of our churches, whether culturally or in terms of their faith journey. The examples outlined in the following chapters should therefore be seen as a catalyst for an achievable evaluation of your own worship setting. Don't see it as yet another time-consuming 'job' to do, but as a revitalizing exercise in developing an integrated spirituality. We hope you will find that this empowers and inspires you, rather than demoralizing you.

Our corporate acts of worship should not be the same as the rest of our lives; rather, they should be the culmination or high-point of our everyday relationships with God—special, set apart, inclusive yet 'transcendent'. In drawing on the biblical 'mountain-top' metaphor, think not only about the experience at the summit, but about the long and winding road that leads there, too. Just as the epiphany experience of Moses at Mount Sinai also included the joy and triumph of the escape from Egypt and the ambiguity and frustration of the desert, similarly our worship should include but transcend our everyday, mundane experiences of life. We hope this book better enables you to reconnect the mundane and the unusual, the immanent experience of God in our everyday lives and the wonderful high-points of corporate celebration, repentance and awe-filled contemplation of our Creator.

TWO

Are you sitting comfortably?

In a culture which is getting ever busier, in which we are ever more bombarded by advertisements and images and in which you can't even wait for a train at some stations or fill up with petrol at some garages without being exposed to TV screens, and in a society which is demanding longer working hours and in which you get less quality time with yourself and others, let alone God, the idea of having 'space' is becoming crucial.

We *need* space—time to contemplate and meditate. In fact, time to *stop* is becoming a rare commodity. Even in our sleep we are processing the busyness of the day and trying to cope with it. Like the TV, it seems almost impossible to switch off.

It is peculiar how many church services mirror the world outside. There is often lots of noise and a degree of general chaos. While of course we desire to be relevant, we also need to be counter-cultural, and in this instance we can counter the culture by promoting the idea of *sacred space*. We can give people the time, the peace, the quiet and the reflection that they just don't get outside—the time for prayer and worship; the time to think about the things that really count. 'Within your temple, O Lord, we meditate on your unfailing love,' writes the psalmist (Psalm 48:9). But do we?

The environment in which we worship is therefore crucial in the process of providing this space for others to 'be'. Perhaps, in the busyness of having to prepare services, of rushing to photocopy music and making sure that there are enough fast choruses to lift the mood and enough slow ones to bring it down again, we forget about *where* we are meeting.

It's time therefore to press 'pause', to think about whether we are really making the most of our 'space' with God. And as we strive for a more holistic approach to worship, it is important to see that the physical and spiritual dimensions to 'space' with God are inseparable. In carving out a physical space in which to worship creatively, we also create spiritual space—in the geographical locality, in our schedules, in the life of the church. We should therefore care about the atmosphere of our place of worship. *Feng shui* may not be everyone's cup of herbal tea, but its popularity has reflected the growing awareness that whether we are relaxing at home or 'creating' at work, our surroundings can have an impact on how we feel and how imaginative we can be.

Since icons and images were smashed in the 'cleansing' of our churches during the English Reformation, Protestants and non-conformists have rather neglected the visual dimension to our worship in favour of the written and spoken word; and this has affected directly how we 'view' the places in which we gather to worship the Creator of all things. Malcom Hamilton has suggested that 'Protestantism divested itself of mystery, miracle and magic. Its conception of God was of an absolutely transcendent being, who, although he had created the world, remained separate from it.'[8] Our places of worship have become more functional, and less about creating a spiritual place in which to experience God.

In seeking to redress this balance, or, more to the point, to find a middle way between immanence and transcendence, some creative worship groups have sought to establish an 'incarnational' approach to theology, which sees—and experiences—God in the things around us, whether that be icons, pictures, music, our natural surroundings, other people, and so on. This differs from an overemphasis on the transcendent God who is 'Other', and the immanent God of the charismatics, for whom an experience with God is very often 'ecstatic'—that is, it is wholly *super*natural. Both of these theological perspectives of course have their valid place; though both tend to deny the physical, holistic side to faith. An overemphasis either way has implications for everything about worship, from the space we occupy to our understanding of the nature of God. It is worth bearing this in mind as we go on to think in this chapter about the theory and practice of space, and in other chapters about the cultural trappings through which we seek to express our worship and our faith.

Welcoming space

For our sins, we are both supporters of Gillingham Football Club. When we travel to 'away' grounds to follow our team, we inevitably make observations about the aspirations of that particular club and its attitude towards visitors, based on our experience of a variety of things such as the price of admission, the quality of facilities, the view we get from our seats and the friendliness of the welcome.

Yet while the football grounds are packed out with worshippers, the same cannot be said for Christian churches. What conclusions will the people in our local communities draw when they visit our places of worship? What will they make of the signs, both literal and metaphorical? The welcome we give or overlook, the interior design, the layout of our worship space and the brand of post-service coffee we serve (or the pub we take them to after—or even for—the service) can speak volumes about our God and the kind of people we want to share our times of worship with. We can indeed reveal much by the thought, time and effort that goes into making the place within which we worship much more inclusive.

Space for each other

The design of the worship space in many of our churches, while functional, tends to put a literal gap and a metaphorical chasm between those who are leading the services and those in the congregation. Whether we intend it or not, a church's layout often sends the message that some people are more important to God than others.

This, of course, is usually unintentional—we believe that we are all equal, that there is 'neither Jew nor Gentile', and so on. Yet, as Christian worship leaders, we also need to search our souls to ask whether such issues betray any deeper theology or aspirations or prejudice. Perhaps, for example, the existing them-and-us arrangement serves our battered egos quite nicely. Let's be honest, many of us musicians yearn for a stage to perform on! But if we are serious about restoring a community focus to our church structures, and if we believe that Christian worship is essentially egalitarian, then careful attention to the layout of our churches can help remove such an us-and-them mentality.

Another associated danger is that we perpetuate the notion that the Church is a detached and aloof institution. Although we should affirm the place of good servant-leadership, we must also remember that people are highly suspicious of groups that preach at them (and the Church has received its fair share of bad press for preaching one thing and doing another). At its worst, a pastor who pontificates from a lofty pulpit can serve to reinforce people's feelings of alienation and subjugation.

As both Principal of Ridley Hall in Oxford and a respected cultural commentator, Graham Cray has commented that '[the postmodern world] is a world distrustful of institutions, hierarchies, centralized bureaucracies and male-dominated organizations. It is a world in which networks and grassroots activities take precedence over large-scale structures and grand designs.'[9] Although it would be foolish to change the way we do things simply to keep in step with public opinion, the crucial thing is to ask why people both outside and inside the Church feel so alienated from institutions, and feel so distrustful of people who claim to have found the truth.

Most of us tend to treat any kind of moral claim with due suspicion, and we can't blame non-Christians for being suspicious of what is going on behind our literally closed doors. While the answer lies perhaps in the level of hypocrisy exercised by many authority figures, both in our private lives and increasingly and importantly in public life too, it is foolish to create more barriers than we need to by neglecting the environment in which we worship God. Whether the public perceives the Church as authoritarian or just plain naff, we must remember that the message we convey comes not just in the form of a sermon, but in the whole package we present.

The Labour Party has benefited of late from root-and-branch reform, and there is no reason to believe that the Church can't, too. Whether we like it or not, the success of the Labour Party's rise to power went hand in hand with a fundamental consideration of its image. From a comprehensive 'colour me beautiful' review of its front-bench stars to incredibly detailed consideration of the colour schemes and layout for its annual conferences and the adoption of the rose as its new symbol, the organization made itself *look* accessible to the people, and put as much work into this as it did into creating new and vibrant policies. It thus positioned itself successfully as 'the People's Party'.

While we acknowledge the dangers intrinsic in placing style over substance, the Labour Party demonstrated the value of not ignoring the medium of the message. And the Church must do likewise. What is the point in having a wonderful message—the message of life itself—if no one really wants to turn up to hear it, either because it seems uninspired or because it actually seems tarnished with a history of corruption and just plain boredom?

We must bear in mind both how we look to outsiders, and how we 'service' the people who are on the inside. Both are equally important. We must look inviting, and we must promise in our appearance and our surroundings something of the creativity of the Creator. And we must try to help our congregations explore and rediscover the spiritual depths within a culture and tradition which often appears devoid of depth or transcendence.

Such lofty ideals necessarily translate into rather mundane decisions. Yet these can crucially affect how our worship communities operate. Alternative worship groups have largely dispensed with linear seating arrangements, for example. Instead, people are encouraged to sit in small groups either around tables, café style, or on cushions on the floor. This creates a welcoming environment, and suggests an air of informality. It suggests that we shall discuss, not just listen. It suggests that we shall make face-to-face contact with each other, not just watch the backs of each other's heads. And it suggests too that we are not in a classroom, but in a place where we shall all contribute (if we want to).

At *Live On Planet Earth* we made a conscious decision to do away with raised platforms too, and let everything happen on one level. Services were predominantly held 'in the round', which meant that those involved in singing, speaking or facilitating discussions or meditations were all physically part of the congregation. The use of different points of focus—for example, a number of screens or microphone positions—allowed us to dispense completely with the notion of a 'front'.

Songs, readings or meditations were led by a team member sitting among the congregation on the floor. We considered ourselves one community and we wanted the layout of the worship space to reflect this. Rather than emphasizing the traditional 'priest versus laity' dichotomy, we wanted to empower the inexperienced churchgoers among our group by emphasizing our commitment to an ethos of the priesthood of all pilgrims.

Importantly, such a style can restore the focus on the relationship between the congregation and God. Worship leaders often exhort the congregation to 'focus on God'; all the while, however, the physical layout of the worship screams, 'Look at me!' So such pleas, for many, fall on deafened ears. Obviously, sitting on the floor is not always suitable for predominantly elderly congregations, although at *LOPE* a lady in her seventies was one of the more regular attenders. The point is that it is possible—even retaining chairs or pews—to think creatively with something as simple as the seating layout, and consequently to alter positively the messages we communicate about ourselves and our God.

Personal space

In recent years there has been a growing shift away from large organizations towards the small and the local. Many successful churches have tried to break up their amorphous congregations, and the growth of cell churches has allowed them to connect with people much more effectively. Group work seems to work best with sets of around ten to fifteen. However, when it comes to worship, it can still be easy to fall into the trap of thinking that big is beautiful. While large-scale expressions of worship can be both reassuring and exhilarating, big congregations afford little opportunity to consider the individual people that comprise the whole.

A small group where honesty is encouraged and trust nurtured can provide an excellent context for a range of authentic, personal responses. People can be more closely involved in the Christian community, and this can help them to be liberated to become more and more active participators in worship, rather than passive receivers.

There is a huge difference between approaches that emphasize the individual and personal. The personal approach integrates the response of each person in relationship with the whole group. David Steindl-Rast has written that 'an individual is defined by what distinguishes it from other individuals. A person is defined by the relationship to others. We are born as individuals, but our task is to become persons, by deeper and more intricate, more highly developed relationships. There is no limit to becoming more truly personal.'[10] Thus the group process creates an environment where we understand and relate to each other better and, con-sequently, where we can worship God more authentically. From a creative worship perspective, small is indeed beautiful.

Sacred space

A common factor in most religions is the tendency to ascribe sacred significance to a given place which then becomes a focus for worship. From the ancient Near Eastern emphasis on mountain-tops (including, of course, the significance attached to these places by the Hebrews) to the druids' sacred circles at Stonehenge, the geography of holiness has always been important. The ongoing land disputes in the Middle East highlight the supreme importance of festival sites such as Jerusalem to the religions of Islam, Judaism and, indeed, Christianity. Even in the 'secular' UK, Christians and non-Christians alike still make pilgrimages to important, sacred sites such as Iona or Canterbury; or beyond our shores to Rome or Lourdes. And we have shown that as a nation, we are willing to create new sites, quasi-spiritual sites too—remember the shrines of remembrance that made Kensington Palace a sacred site for those mourning the death of Diana, Princess of Wales, in 1997.

Many of us respond intuitively to the notion of certain places being imbued with sacred significance. And though we might want to temper this with the new-covenant Christian understanding of God as immanent and accessible to all, it is certainly worthwhile to reclaim something of the metaphorical and symbolic understanding of sacred space. While we believe that Jesus has 'broken through the curtain', we still recognize the idea of coming to meet with God, and the symbolic and spiritual value invested by God in the Temple helps us to understand the significance of this.

As already mentioned, an overemphasis on the transcendent God meant that in the past we neglected the ambience of our worship spaces and let functionality rule. However, the (mainly) charismatic emphasis on immanence—the idea that we have an ongoing 'personal relationship with Jesus'—though healthy, has also helped to take away from the sense of awe and wonder with which we can approach God. Such theology *can* suggest that God is more of a pal than the supreme holy being; our songs have emphasized the feeling that Jesus is more of a boyfriend than the second member of the Trinity; and our places of worship have led to the feeling that it just doesn't matter about our surroundings because 'you can worship God anywhere—even in the toilet'. In fact, in some church movements (including the ones we personally grew up in), which boast of spiritual encounters and signs and wonders, it can rarely feel 'spiritual' at all. Many services lack a sense of meditation, contemplation, awe or holiness.

In our version of the Labyrinth, we make every effort to infer the notion that it is in some way a symbol of a sacred encounter with a holy God. The congregation are encouraged to remove their shoes and socks. This not only allows people to perceive the ground as symbolically sacred and mysterious, it also encourages them to develop a sensory, tactile relationship with their environment. The Western human being has become increasingly removed from his and her natural surroundings; we are cocooned. By encouraging tactility, we can facilitate a deeper sense of our belonging to the cosmos and the created order, and consequently promote a more caring attitude to creation, more reverence for the Creator and a greater sense of our becoming fully human in Christ.

Many people who have walked the Labyrinth have spoken of the way in which they have tangibly experienced a sense of sacred space within its boundaries. Perhaps by rethinking and designing what have often become over-familiar worship areas, we can rediscover an appreciation of the sacred within our services.

There is no reason why your worship necessarily must be indoors, either. In one of the charismatic churches we used to attend, one of the more inspirational events of the week was a regular prayer meeting which was held early each Saturday morning in the local woods. We met on a hill, from where we could see the beauty of creation as we prayed to the Creator.

At *LOPE*, we would also sometimes meet outside. We once

gathered to observe the summer solstice—not, as you might think, in the fashion of a druid festival, but as an acknowledgment as created beings of the incredible 'createdness' of our planet and its Creator. And although the sunrise was obscured by cloud, again the experience of worshipping God in the context of being within creation was profound.

Back inside, having no chairs enabled us to be more experimental in getting people to move around physically during a service; it was relatively simple to get people to organize themselves into small discussion or prayer groups, or to move to a 'station' or icon located in a particular area. Additionally many alternative worship groups make use of contemplation and meditation, which is best undertaken when people are able to find some space in which to relax—perhaps by lying on the floor, or moving around in the case of 'body prayers'. Without room to move, this kind of activity tends to prove impossible.

A worship space can be designed around the notion of easy movement and access to various areas or installations. When there are no physical obstacles, we have found that people tend to be much more willing to move metaphorically out of their 'safety zones' and actively participate in the service. This, in turn, encourages a more creative mentality on the part of those planning services; if you know that people are more likely to respond to something out of the ordinary, you will be far more inclined to 'try it' in the service.

Groups such as *Grace* pay careful attention to the layout and design of the worship space as they place considerable importance on the creation of a conducive environment and an atmosphere which helps the congregation to relax. The hope is that this in turn enables people to be creative, participative and real in their worship. The methods used to create this ambience can vary tremendously. For example, the use of soft lighting and relaxing music (see Chapter 5) can do much to relax the congregation. Some creative worship groups and services make a direct attempt to mimic the 'feel' of a chill-out room in a nightclub. Such rooms are set away from the pulsating lights, lasers and beats of the dance floor, in another part of the building. They have mellow lighting and comfortable chairs; there will probably be some gentle, ambient music playing; and such rooms allow clubbers to unwind from the intensity of the dance area, to sip some water and recharge their batteries.

For others, like us, whose social circles revolved more around other settings such as pubs, cafés or dinner parties, these too can be adapted for a service. Groups such as *Free House* in Cheltenham and *Holy Joes* in Buckingham Palace Road, Victoria, meet in back rooms in pubs. The point is not that all churches should try to be like pubs and clubs. Rather, by creating a suitable atmosphere in the light of the style and content of the particular service you are aiming to facilitate and the people that you are working with, you can go a long way to enabling them to 'be themselves' and consequently produce a creative, worshipping environment.

More than this, however, the design of the worship space can be a highly creative and worshipful activity in and of itself. While, for many, the thought of having to encourage a lethargic congregation to participate in its design may seem like a difficult task, it can, if correctly framed, be a wonderful and liberating experience. You only have to see the interest in TV programmes like 'Changing Rooms' to realize how much we love to tweak the design of the places where we live and move and have our being.

The wider point is to see the value in embracing the creative process as part of our worship. If we are willing to make the point explicitly that the preparation is part of the worship itself, then we can go a long way to making sacred, and therefore valuing, such work. At *LOPE* it was the contributions of all the team that helped to create a worship space that at times was thoroughly awe-inspiring. We hope you will discover that a little effort goes a long, long way.

THREE

Focusing in

Few inventions have turned the world on as much as the television. From the *favelas* of São Paulo to the penthouses of New York, 'the box' has fully pervaded our lives. So much so, that in the civil wars of both the former Yugoslavia and the Soviet Union, one of the recurring prime targets was the TV centres—most famously when Nato bombed and destroyed the national studios in Belgrade. TVs, CPUs, VCRs and VDUs—not books—have become the weapons of the contemporary revolution. Control the visual media and you win the war, whether it's Serb versus Croat or Coke versus Pepsi.

Alongside this technological revolution comes a cultural coup of equal significance. For more than two centuries, the 'modern', 'enlightened' Western world placed its confidence in science and reason, and dismissed religion as mere superstition. The modern 'project' both promoted and was enabled by language, following on from the invention of the printing press. Philosophers such as René Descartes, Friedrich Nietzsche and Immanuel Kant declared that humanity was moving inexorably onwards and upwards to better and brighter things. At the same time, the Industrial Revolution helped to forge an incredibly confident attitude among the rapidly developing European nations.

During the twentieth century, such an optimistic worldview came under pressure. As the progress of humanity and its big ideas were undermined by the World Wars, ecological catastrophe and so on, so too was the trust in rationality and objective, scientifically verifiable 'truth'. Like the story of the king in his birthday suit, once we finally dared to expose them, the big stories or 'meta-narratives' no longer seemed so plausible. Consequently, the reliability of the vehicle by which they were conveyed— language—became subject to increasing scepticism.

The concepts promoted by the great thinkers of the modern era were 'deconstructed' by postmodernists such as Jacques Derrida, Jean Baudrillard, Michel Foucault and Jean-François Lyotard, who claimed that language was inherently untrustworthy, that words reveal little more than the hidden agenda of the author and that they have no real meaning in and of themselves. After all, when you try to find what a word means, you go to your dictionary—which simply refers you to more words.

While you may think that such abstract and extreme theories do not affect us, the ordinary people on the street, they have in fact filtered down from the dusty halls of academia through the education system and (particularly) the media into our everyday lives. We have the twin cultural experience of becoming used to pictures instead of words, while at the same time becoming more cynical and suspicious about the 'truth claims' made by the never-ending flow of extravagant and outlandish advertising. Within this developing culture of suspicion, why should people be any more impressed by our Christian claims? The fact is, they aren't. Like Thomas, they want to see the holes and touch the wounds. They want experience, not dogma.

Within the modern era, reasoned apologetics and stirring sermons provided the best method of communication for the Church to spread its message of good news and for people to 'meet with God'. But the world, as we have seen, has undergone massive changes since such methods were most effective; yet all the while, church services continue to use, by and large, these didactic methods of communication—the teaching, preaching and even the prayers reflect a preoccupation with language and words.

Of course, invaluable work has been done by the Church and its theologians in defending the claims of the 'Good Book' and the truth contained within it. We do not wish to lose a sense of objectivity about the Bible and its narratives. And yet the way in which people tend to respond to images in today's society—

allowing them to work on their own levels, reading into and responding to them as best they can, not in any right or wrong way, but subjectively—is liberating.

Visuals, as well as stories and rituals (which are dealt with in the following chapters), avoid the extravagant claims of 'objective' language; instead, we interact with them simply and personally. They work in different ways with different people; we are left to make up our own minds rather than having to accept the received 'wisdom' of others.

It may be tempting to dismiss this as a 'youth thing' or as a passing whim or phase. Yet if we believe that what is happening is something much more significant, it can point us to the conclusion that, for much more profound reasons, visuals are one of the most powerful tools of communication at this point in history.

Getting the picture

People are becoming increasingly alienated by the Church's intransigence. They yearn for an experience that takes them beyond the mundane, for transcendence, and they desperately seek spirituality—while church attendance figures, which have slipped gradually since the 1850s, have begun to drop even more dramatically in the last two decades. Clearly there are complex forces behind this, but there are good reasons why worship and experience can offer new and exciting ways of reversing the trend. People are no longer asking 'Is this true?' but 'Does this work?'; they are looking for an 'epiphany', an experience of God, and worship is the place where this might happen.

In Christian worship, visuals afford us a plurality of opportunities to connect with God. Imagine, instead of an hour-long sermon on the work of atonement, instead (or at least, alongside!) gazing at Francisco de Zurbarán's wonderful painting, *Bound Lamb*. It allows you to consider and react to the idea of Jesus as the helpless, sacrificial lamb in a far more emotive, personal, inexplicable (and thus soulful) way than words can express. The director of the National Gallery, Neil MacGregor, recently explained why he decided to put together an exhibition of different artistic portrayals of Christ (the *Seeing Salvation* exhibition). He is worth quoting at length:

Luther would have argued, I think, that the reason you have to focus on the word rather than the image is because the word is certain and clear and univalent and the image is necessarily ambiguous and therefore cannot confidently lead you to truth. Well, not many of us now think that language can do that, either; it's a notion of language that is completely unsustainable... The extraordinary thing about works [of art] is that they offer you a completely other way of organizing the world and asking the questions. I think people are very quickly aware of that, and very quickly enriched, and I think there's an enormous desire, and a real possibility, to go back to that.[11]

For many people, visuals will 'speak' far more eloquently and powerfully in worship than any construction of words. Not only are they culturally more conducive, but when we are encouraging people to connect with the mysterious and transcendent God, they offer a more realistic and honest medium through which to seek to interact with the divine.

Whether it's Salvador Dali's deeply moving *Christ of Saint John of the Cross* or a simple picture portraying the beauty of creation, visuals can feed the process of making worship less wordy and precise, and more subjective, experiential and, as a consequence, relevant. Letting go of this objective wordiness and embracing subjective visual media can be a scary experience, especially for those of us whose roots are sunk in the word-based Christian world. But if we really care about the the unchurched majority, we are faced with a substantial and hugely exciting challenge to move our worship away from *our* world of books and language towards *their* world of visuals and experience.

It is also worth considering how people best remember information and ideas. Think how many sermons you recall in detail. Then think how many television advertisements you remember, even for products that are no longer sold. While we all respond differently to different learning styles, in general we take in much more of what we see and hear in comparison with what we simply hear or read. The best combination for retaining information is that of watching and listening at the same time, hence the effectiveness and costliness of television advertising. While churches are not teaching people to retain information for exams, and we would resist arguments based on pure pragmatism, such considerations add weight to the idea that worship spaces should be made much more visually stimulating.

The following is an outline of some of the ways alternative and creative worship groups have used visuals in their worship. It is not exhaustive, nor is it intended to be definitive, but rather, as with the rest of this book, it can be used a stepping-stone. Most groups tend to create or use a darkened worship space which allows them to use projected pictures.

First, you can use slides. We tend to use them in two ways. One is as a combination of pictures or slogans specifically to illustrate a point—it's quite easy to print out a slogan or soundbite on a word processor, and photograph it onto slide film; useful phrases in a talk can be backed up visually, and can prove much more aesthetically pleasing than an overhead projector. The other is as a visual backdrop to add aesthetic beauty. There is nothing like preparing people's hearts before the service by projecting something like (for example) a huge red heart on to a drape of muslin. Think of how such an image can work for different people: some may be feeling that their heart is broken, and they need to meet with God to experience healing. Some may feel their heart pounding in anticipation of sensing the Spirit of God. Others may respond by considering how the heart represents God's enormous love for them, despite everything. Still others may simply consider their loneliness, or their love for someone else. If you don't have a slide of a heart, get someone creative to paint one—and photograph it.

Sometimes we use visuals to juxtapose or play with a theme. They can provoke a response and work as a great discussion-starter. Imagine the drama of preparing your congregation to think about the omnipotence of God by showing a picture of Holocaust survivors from Auschwitz, for example, or famine victims in Ethiopia. In the average church context, you might have to be sensitive to the ways in which you use such images. But be careful not to 'explain' too much if you can help it.

Taking photos yourself can help to provide a local flavour. Cranbrook, the town in which *Live On Planet Earth* was based, has a beautiful windmill. From time to time we would project pictures of the mill, or our high street, or local scenes, when asking people to think or pray about the issues on our own doorstep.

As well as creating your own slides, you can also explore images available on slide at most cathedrals and art galleries. Check out copyright restrictions—although most places allow free usage in a non-profit-making context. Be creative!

Second, try video clips. You might use an episode from a film to illustrate a theme; or play a short excerpt from a TV pro-gramme.[12] Soap operas in particular are for ever exploring themes that we should be thinking about in church, whether adultery, or Aids, or the difficulties of single parenthood, and so on. They can help show where our society is 'at', or lift the mood, or simply provide a welcome distraction from a long talk.

In one service, we were thinking about the challenge of being a radical Christian; so we used a clip from the film *Point Break*, in which the hero jumps out of a plane without a parachute to catch another character who has one—a bit extreme, but it worked well as a highly memorable illustration of the point we were making about taking risks for God! Such an image helps to make the connection so much more effectively than a clever use of words.

If you can't find a clip to illustrate your theme, why not get a drama group to take a camcorder and produce a short film themselves? We did, and it seemed to work. Or take the camcorder out to your local shopping centre and find out what the community around you think about a particular issue, or what things concern them most, or what they think of church. It's a great way to help inform your prayers.

Third, video 'loops'. You can produce a repeating loop of a short video sequence, which people can then meditate on for a few minutes. For example, a clip of water droplets falling into a pool can help you think about the refreshing of the Holy Spirit—or the ripples that one small drop in the ocean can actually make. You could loop images either from a nature programme—one of our favourites was of a chrysalis turning into a butterfly—or, better still, created by yourself with a camcorder.

Most groups and churches have someone who spends their life in their garden shed tinkering with suitcases full of electronic technology. And they're usually delighted to be brought on board. Even for technophobes, it is fairly straightforward: link two VCRs with a scart lead, put a blank tape in VCR 1 and the tape with the clip you want to loop on VCR 2. Press record on VCR 1 and play on VCR 2, then, when you come to the end of the clip, pause VCR 1 and stop and rewind VCR 2. Then just repeat the process a few times! The end result is a loop as long as you want, to act as an ideal focus or backdrop for any given service.

We ran a series of services looking at the 'four elements'. For the one on water, we sent out someone with a camcorder to video a tap running, a local stream, puddles, a bath and whatever else they could find. We then produced a loop for the service. For fire, we recorded a candle burning—which is easier, as you can just leave the camera recording for an hour. Or you could record a bonfire burning from start to finish. A video projection of something like a candle burning can speak volumes about light-and-dark symbolism, or the fire of the Spirit, and so on. If you are stuck, groups such as *Grace* (see the Appendix of Resources) have produced videos packed full of useful clips. But it would be better to produce your own, even if it's not so polished—remember, the process is part of the worship.

Similarly you could get hold of an old cine-projector or Hi8 and loop some images. These create a very evocative, 'retro' feel.

Fourth, computer graphics. If you're really keen on computers or you have someone in your church who is, why not get them to produce graphics generated on a computer to illustrate a theme? Get them to bring along their PC and hook it up to a video projector, if you have one, or just a network of TV sets. You would need to purchase a special converter, which translates images from a PC in a format that can be used on a TV or video projector. If used tastefully, such images can be an excellent aid to worship. And you can always project the text for any songs or poems you might be using in the service. Again, it's far more hip than the OHP!

Fifth, banners and backdrops. Not a new idea, but again an excellent opportunity to be creative. Get a group of people to design some banners or backdrops that illustrate recurring themes for your church or group. We made some that reflected the particular concerns of many people within our group about global poverty, as well as creation and ecological issues. You could design a logo for your service or church. Think of some of the key Christian symbols, and how these could be creatively portrayed. For example, some artists involved with *LOPE* produced some wonderful banners, one of which symbolized the resurrection using the cross, contrasting the night of death on one side of the cross with the sunrise of new life on the other. The cross is an obvious example; others that might be used in this context are fire, the dove, the lamb or the fish.

More obscure examples that we have used include the wild goose, which symbolizes the Spirit in the Celtic tradition (instead of the dove). This is a good example of recontextualizing the

Christian symbols and creating your own. Think about why it is that the goose was a better symbol for Celtic Christians than the dove; then think what alternative takes you could come up with, that reflect the culture around you.

We also portrayed some of our other passions in life. Several of us are surfers, and so we used the imagery of the sea and waves combined with Christian themes of God as Creator. It all helps us to feel like we are worshipping from within our culture. Perhaps you would want to incorporate something of the issues concerning the wider community in your area. These backdrops can then be draped around your worship space, creating a colourful collage of artwork that reminds you as a group or church of your identity, vision and mission. Again, resist the temptation to use too many words, and avoid overloading the worship space with images. Let the pictures speak for themselves and let them be powerful images that move people to reach for and cry out to their Creator in worship and prayer.

Visuals at their best are simple and egalitarian. The power of visuals, images and icons can be undermined by over-explanation. They work best if you resist the temptation to make sure everyone knows exactly what you are trying to convey. Understanding this can help you to choose your visuals carefully. Ideally, you want something simple that can appeal to different people on different levels. Like Jesus' use of parables, the power of such stories or narratives is in the hearer or viewer internalizing and processing them. When a child is struggling to find the answer to a question, it can be very tempting to shout it out for them—the true teacher takes time to stand back and is not afraid of the silence of indecision.

FOUR

The writing's on the wall

We established in the previous chapter that language and words have lost the power to convey empirical 'truth' in the cut-and-dried way that people once thought they could. But of course, we need to qualify this, in case you think that we take a vow of silence in our services. Words do, in fact, play an integral part in our own lives and in our worship (after all, we're writing a book). It is the *over-use* of words and the unrealistic trust and dependence we placed on them that has now gone, and we believe that this can be a positive thing.

Words can sometimes best be used to *describe*, not *prescribe*—as with great works of poetry and fiction. A poem of very few words by someone like John Donne, for instance, can help unlock profound spiritual truths. Just because it may not 'scientifically' report fact, as we might imagine a historical document to, it can still contain truth about life, the 'truth' that can help to set us free. In the same way, you may get more from a story—whether it's *The Pilgrim's Progress* or Harry Potter—than from a Christian paperback about 'how you must live'. While the Harry Potter books are controversial in Christian circles for their inclusion of magic and witches, they nevertheless raise issues of spirituality which have clearly struck a chord not only with children but with adults. Within our postmodern context, the place of 'story' has taken on a renewed significance.

Selective memories

Take those historical documents, just mentioned. Perhaps forty years ago, it was assumed that historical events could be reported and recorded in an unbiased, factual account. This is how it happened—end of story. Now, however, there is less trust in the concept of 'history', because even if we have all the facts to hand, we realize that they can be used selectively. There are usually at least two sides to every story. Consider the teaching of the Second World War in schools across the world. Many people have been brought up in Britain to believe that there were the goodies—the 'British'—and the baddies, the Germans. But it's unlikely that the Chinese and Japanese, the Americans and Russians, the Italians and the French told the story in that way. We see the world through tinted glasses, from our own perspectives. No two people are likely to tell the same story of history, as it 'actually' was, because we are all players in that history, and we have our own background, our own presuppositions, our own take or spin on every event.

This can be a liberating realization, as we can then hold less strongly to our modernistic desire for verifiable, objective facts, and instead understand that we all have stories about how we organize the world and how things happened—not only in terms of actual events, but in terms of the huge questions of life. Who am I? How did I get here? How come there's evil in the world? Does God exist?

In the past, many Christians have looked to the Bible as a purely factual account of history which, in turn, explains these big questions of life. So, the world was made in six days. Noah's flood covered the whole earth. And Jonah was a real man who was swallowed by a real big whale. We forgot the fact that these accounts were written at a specific time by a specific people to describe their own predicament, their own answers to the big questions of their lives. Many of the stories that we have read as fact were never meant to be 'factual accounts' as we would understand the phrase, but instead were ways of telling the story of Israel, and of conveying theological truths in the genres of the time. (We also note that they were written from Israel's perspective. We in Britain may find the idea of 'marching into the promised land' comforting; but imagine how a Palestinian

Christian in the occupied territories might consider it in a different way.)

And yet, we believe that the stories of the Bible contain truth. And they involve the real people of Israel who lived real lives and were guided by God through exodus to the promised land, then into exile and back again. These people saw themselves as characters within a bigger story; these were the ones who explained how they came to be weeping by the rivers of Babylon. As Christians, we believe that they played a crucial part in the story of life, comprising the all-important 'first half' of God's involvement in the world. But we must remember that the Israelites did not record 'history' as we have come to understand the word—that was never their intention.

The Old Testament also has a wealth of stories involving real people, who were colourful characters in gripping plots. Even though we believe that much of the Old Testament recounts historical fact, it is still written in a beautiful poetic and lyrical way. Many of its books are acclaimed critically as great works of literature in their own right, and we miss much of their value if we read them simply as 'history'. There is purpose to be unlocked within these narratives. The wonderful tales of exodus and exile—the account of our 'salvation history'—is not a list of dos and don'ts of the Jewish or Christian faith, but a series of well-crafted stories about God's involvement with the world.

In a different way, the Psalms describe lyrically the whole of life's experiences—not just the triumphal ones, but those of physical suffering, *angst*, pain, the feeling of being abandoned by God. They are works of poetry and song that contain a theological understanding about the whole range of human life. Their power lies not in the fact that they 'tell it how it is', but in the feeling and emotion that are packed into the lyrics. In the same way that we respond to a beautiful love song today, so we respond to the poetic power of the Psalms, and less to the objective facts about faith. (It is always a dangerous move to take one psalm and expound upon its contents without referring to others. It is all well and good to base a sermon on the merits of Psalm 1, which says that 'the Lord watches over the way of the righteous' [v. 6]. But pity the new convert who then turns to Psalm 88, only to read that 'I am set apart with the dead... whom you remember no more' [v. 5].) Other books, such as Job, Lamentations and the Song of Songs, all draw lyrically on the fullness of the human experience in a way that was never meant to be 'factual' *per se*, but which describes the highs and lows of our humanity and our relationship with God.

As we have said, we affirm that the Bible recounts the real events of real people who also told stories about who they were and where they came from. You have a mixture, if you like, of 'fact' and 'fiction'. As we move into the New Testament, we see historically verifiable events taking place, which give us confidence that this is not all a product of someone's imagination. Jesus did exist. The disciples were real, and spread the gospel across their known world. Many of them died horrible deaths for the sake of it.

But consider the way in which Jesus sought to teach people about the facts of life, so to speak. Rarely did he tell things 'the way they were'. Instead, he spoke in stories—parables—and, much to our modernist chagrin, he was reluctant to explain them. Like the pictures and images we thought about in Chapter 2, Jesus allowed these stories to work for people on their own levels. He spoke them, but left others to interpret. They were told for those who had ears to hear. They weren't puzzles or riddles which had a right or wrong answer. They were ways of explaining what, in particular, the Kingdom of God was really like.

In the same way, as Christians in the twenty-first century, we affirm that there are certain verifiable 'truths' about the Christian story that we hold to. We base our belief around the actual existence of the Israelites, their prophets and kings, and crucially around Jesus and his disciples and the writers of the New

Testament. And yet we have a duty to retell stories about the Kingdom of God for a new generation—to unlock the wonderful depths of the Bible afresh, in a way that does not just ask, 'Did this, or didn't this, happen?' but, 'What can this tell us about life and our relationship with God?'

Telling stories

We personally used stories at *Live On Planet Earth*, whether they were taken from the Bible or written by members of the team or the congregation. There is power in recounting one of Jesus' parables and, like he did, letting it stand alone, unexplained. You can always follow up a parable in a midweek discussion or a small-group session later in the service. But to demonstrate the power of the stories by not explaining them is telling enough.

There will be several people in your church who write poetry. They may not have admitted it to you, but they'll be there. The creativity we helped nurture at *LOPE* simply by inviting people to write poems around a theme was deeply moving. We tended to project the words up with computer graphics, and read them— sometimes all together, as a form of liturgy. With the right kind of background music and lighting, the effect of a well-performed poem in such a group is astonishing. It nurtures creativity not only among the writers, but among the hearers or readers. It takes time and effort and imagination to respond to a poem—just as it takes time, effort and imagination to respond to a parable. It is not always easy. But it provides an entirely different discipline from listening to a 'how to' sermon. Most significantly, it demands a personal, imaginative response from the hearer. It demands creative, spiritual interaction.

We wrote this short poem as a prelude to communion in a service that we ran on the theme of hospitality, on giving and receiving—on our relationship with the provider God, who in turn lets us provide for him, in two-way relationship.

The Guest

Jesus himself was a guest at a wedding in Cana—
we've heard it all before.
He turned the water into wine. (It's our proof-text against puritans.)
Vintage stuff.
Jesus was a guest—of humanity.
The heavenly host, who laid on a harvest of abundance for the world,
the creator, my provider, became the guest
of the animals in the stable,
the villagers of Nazareth,
the religious leaders in the Temple,
the prostitutes, drunkards, tax collectors.
He let us play host, did away with the VIP pass,
ate, drank, and was probably merry.
Became one of us, dined at our table.
Ate the same bread, drank the same wine—
everybody having a good time.
Shared stories;
shared our story.

When he left the table,
he left bread and wine.
He himself left,
but he left himself.
The guest,
once more,
became the consummate Host.

When it comes to talks and sermons, we have sometimes found ourselves being accused of not providing the 'meat'—the half-hour sermon that seems obligatory at every church. *Grace* tends not to use sermons at all. If there is a subject to be explored, it uses group discussion as the forum. It is fair to say, however, that with complex subjects the input from a well-read 'expert' can be invaluable. At *LOPE* we would combine group discussion with a series of usually two or three succinct talks of around five or ten minutes each. We tackled a given subject by trying to outline differing perspectives on it, combined with the biblical background, and then allowing the congregation to discuss them. Among our team we had a number of graduate and postgraduate theologians, and we always tried to encourage all who attended our services to think through issues for themselves—we tried hard not to impose a 'party line'. (For some of us, the questioning that is an intrinsic part of this new approach to church and worship led us to want to study theology formally.)

So, for example, in a series of services on sexuality, we looked at the issue of homosexuality. We avoided being overly prescriptive on the subject (for which we upset some and heartened others), but set out a range of theological ideas and allowed the congregation in small groups to discuss their own views and the merits of the various theologies on offer. There was no right or wrong answer, but an attempt to provide some of the theological tools to think further about such an issue—and to encourage people to do exactly that for themselves, in relationship with others.

This reflected our efforts to try to promote a bottom-up form of Christian community rather than a top-down, authoritarian one. We tried in all areas of the service to ensure the involvement of the whole community. So, in this context, we would try to allow for an ongoing discussion-based forum for such an issue. And the music, prayers, symbolic acts, imagery and meditations would combine to allow people to engage with God in worship as they responded to some of the points that were raised.

Theme-based services help to connect more effectively with the real lives of the congregation. We found that people responded well to issues that affected them and others they cared for—issues such as self-image, ecology, poverty, death, sex and drugs, and so on. They were encouraged to relate their faith to these areas, and to see how, in a small way, they could help to change the world through helping to change their locality. We always tried to see the service as a whole, avoiding the distinction between a cerebral sermon and an experiential 'worship time', and trying to integrate any words or talks as part of our worship.

As well as short bursts of teaching, we would from time to time use meditations and monologues—written or spoken thoughts or musings—to help people think further about things within a more deliberately worshipful atmosphere. The written or spoken word need not be used simply to tell people what they must think. If used creatively and sensitively, people enjoy the use of words. When we specifically asked for the involvement of the whole congregation, for example in responding to God in the face of suffering, we would typically provide a number of different media through which they could work. One of these would be writing. Those who felt inclined could create a poem, a piece of prose, a rant or any other form of written response. This is one example, a poem by a young person written during a service on the theme of creativity:

Lying in my darkness
I am a traveller.
Fly by wire to catch your rays—
Flying out from the mirrorball of your Spirit
I catch the rays,
Fill the world with light.
With all the freedom, the knowledge, the opportunity,
We are nothing until we catch a beam of your light,
A spark to light a fire in my eyes.
My heart, help me burn!

Take me to the highest mountain and I will take your name there;
Take me to the coldest blue ocean
And swim with me.

Your creation is so vast:
Create with me,
Live through me,
And I will create with you.

Paint the world with bristles of belief,
With colours of peace and love and life.
I know you feel with us;
Emotion lives with you
And you give it a place in all of our hearts.

Words cannot possibly have a place here:
Silence is powerful alone.
You speak with me in my silence,
You speak to others through my silence
Where words are nothing.

Words,
Deeds,
Love.
The greatest of these is love.

At LOPE we had three largish contingents of young people: one group came from a nearby boarding school, another comprised the local church youth groups and the third was a group who came as a result of a drop-in centre we ran in the locality. These groups varied tremendously in terms of academic ability and understanding, but in using varied forms of speaking and writing, and encouraging a mixture of personal responses through art, modelling clay, writing and so on, we tried to allow all to participate and to respond to God without feeling marginalized or excluded.

Is the writing on the wall for language and words? It often was, literally, in our services—projected in giant letters into the darkness. But the beauty and depth of language that is used properly can help to unlock the treasures of our faith that, for too long, have stayed trapped in the vaults of modernity. We should use it wisely.

FIVE

Sounding out

Music can have a tremendous impact upon us all. It not only affects our moods, making us happy, aggressive, relaxed, excited or sad, but perhaps unlike any other art form, it can really touch our soul. Not surprisingly, it has accompanied religious worship throughout the world and is widely believed to contribute to an openness and receptivity towards spiritual encounters. While recognizing that music is a powerful tool that should be used carefully in the context of worship, we should also see it as a true aid to touching the divine, and be as colourful, creative and diverse as we possibly can.

Like any other cultural manifestation, music does not take place in a vacuum. Its use in any communal setting tends to reflect the worldview, social status and preferences of the predominant or most powerful people within a group. For example, the style of music played in a café or pub communicates both the desired clientele and the musical preferences of the management. Similarly, within churches the style of music tends to reflect the customs and cultural preferences of the leadership and it can communicate a clear message about who will be welcome across our thresholds.

Music can become a highly significant factor in defining ourselves as people and the cultural tribe we identify with or 'belong' to. Similarly, groups of all kinds can be defined by their musical preferences. In the Sixties, you were a mod if you liked the Small Faces or a rocker if you were into the Rolling Stones. And you'd wear the hairstyle and the clothes to go with the cultural package. In the Seventies, you were a punk if you were into the Sex Pistols, or a skinhead if you were into a ska band such as the Specials. Music, fashion and identity have become almost inextricably linked within youth culture.

In contemporary society, musicians can become hugely famous

and culturally influential even if they seem not to be that talented! Take Nelson Mandela's meeting with the Spice Girls. On the one hand we had a powerful political leader who had affected people across the world and had been imprisoned in his struggle, and on the other a random collection of previously unknown singers. It is not only remarkable that such an encounter might take place, but for Mandela to say that this was the 'best day of his life' reveals how highly we esteem musicians, both socially and culturally.

As a result, for aficionados, music can assume what seems to others to be an unusual importance. In the Church, musical preferences have become an important issue and a battleground through which power struggles have been manifest, as groups vie for priority to be given to their favoured style. In the 'renewal movement' of the Sixties and Seventies, for instance, one of the major issues involved whether a church played choruses or sang hymns. For some, that is still the case today. But for alternative worshippers, the music of the former 'revolution' seems stuck in a Sixties and Seventies timewarp. This has been intensified by the fact that musical styles and fashions change at a much higher pace than they ever used to, and have fragmented into ever increasing subcultures.

So how can we find a constructive and productive way forward that means that we use music positively? As already suggested, all communal music, including that used in churches, is a cultural and social statement. We might think of it in terms of which radio station a particular congregation may reflect in its taste. Some might incorporate choirs, organ music and classical pieces— suggesting an affinity with, and an invitation to, Classic FM listeners. Others might go for a more 'easy listening' approach with choruses of varying kinds, perhaps reflecting Radio 2 devotees. Other churches with younger leaders might use a musical style that accords with typical Radio 1 listeners (still a long way away from what a lot of 'young people' actually listen to—but that's another story!).

The point is not to denigrate any particular musical tradition but rather to highlight the fact that the music we use in our services is always 'enculturated'—that is, it reflects a cultural format that is present in the wider world. This usually embodies the preferred listening of the dominant group within the congregation. For people who feel a close affinity with another genre of music (indeed, which might be a central factor in helping to form their very identity), to find themselves in a context where their own taste in music is at best ignored or at worst denigrated will represent a considerable block to worship and may cause them to feel alienated within the church community. This sociological observation forms a base, which, once grasped, can help us along the road to using music more effectively in our services.

Of course, music within our services need not be more 'trendy' for the sake of it. Rather, as churches we should try to ensure that the music we use is *authentic*—both to our congregations and to those outside our churches whom we are hoping to attract. Furthermore, it will be impossible for us to reach out effectively to people within our community unless we actively take steps to incorporate their culture(s) within our worship, or embrace the culture of those who are already involved. Music is a particularly potent and tangible expression of culture, and consequently it must form an integral part of any attempt to encourage an encounter with God through worship for people outside our usual congregations. Note the qualification here: we should not use music simply to get people into the church; we should use it to allow those people to worship more authentically once they have come in.

There have been occasions in the history of the Church in this country when efforts have been made to connect the music used in worship to that found in wider culture. For example, some of the hymn writers of the eighteenth and nineteenth centuries adapted 'pub tunes' of the time to be used in chapels and evangelistic meetings. Additionally, the Salvation Army, with its roots among working-class people, used brass band music to make a similar connection with the man and woman on the street. Sadly, in the last three decades the Church has had a poor level of interaction with contemporary culture and particularly with so-called secular music. Books such as *Pop Goes the Gospel* promoted alarmist extremism, suggesting that anything but worship music was at best 'dodgy' and at worst satanic; and consequently they have left a terrible legacy of dualism in our thinking and theology, such that many evangelicals feel compelled to distinguish between 'Christian' and 'secular' music.

When we set up *Live On Planet Earth*, one of the defining factors in encouraging us was that the music in our churches bore no relation to the music we loved—the soundtrack to our lives. The music outside the church was, to most people of our age, a crucial part of our lives. Many Christians, not only 'teenagers' but people in their twenties and thirties and those from ethnic minorities, continue to be frustrated with this situation, and, as the statistics show, many more simply walk away from church. While the mass exodus cannot be blamed entirely on the style of music, this is nevertheless a great example of the failure of Christian worship to connect with the lives of so many people. If we truly believe that music forms an integral part of our identity, especially among young people, and if we also believe that music can lift the soul and help us encounter the divine, then to avoid helping people to worship with music they love is simply foolishness.

Those who remain can sometimes find it difficult to connect 'church' to everyday life. Christian worship should not mimic mainstream culture for the sake of it, but when we fail funda-mentally to engage or connect with people's cultural identity, we thwart the idea of holism. So, at *LOPE* we actively pursued the ideal that our whole lives should be seen as an ongoing act of worship to God. We wanted to encourage and to model the possibility of living integrated, whole lives, to be 'in the world but not of it'. We didn't want to immerse ourselves in a separatist Christian subculture that turns its back on the world. But how can you do this and remain 'in the world' at all?

Church is not primarily meant to be entertaining, but the more Christian worship includes some synthesis with the worshippers' daily lives, the more they are likely to identify with the call to see their whole lives as an act of worship. The biblical narratives, both in the old and new covenants, never really had to address such complexities, but it is clear that, culturally speaking, there was little disparity between the music used in everyday life and that used in the worship context. It is also clear that expressions of worship evolved to encompass the changing situations of both the Israelites and the early Church—for example, to accommodate the move from the mobile tabernacle to the fixed site of the Temple in Jerusalem. The early Church initially met in homes and 'upper rooms' and later in secret, hidden places to avoid persecution from emperors such as Nero and Domitian. Until the beginnings of the institutionalization of the Church under Constantine, Christian expressions of worship were inextricably rooted in the language and daily lives of 'the people'.

From despair to where?

It is clear from the Psalms, Ecclesiastes and Lamentations that Jewish worship encompassed lament and complaint as well as joyous celebration. It reflected the gamut of experience, from expressions of the mundane to glorious high points such as the song of Moses and Miriam after the exodus escape (Exodus 15:1–21). Indeed, one of the common complaints against the people of Israel by prophets such as Isaiah (1:10–17), Hosea (6:6–10), Micah (6:6–8) and Amos (5:18–24) are acts of worship (sacrifices) that are not grounded in lives of worship. This is a theme Jesus takes up in his attacks on the Pharisees in Matthew 23.

For people whose lives are characterized by despair, whether as a result of physical hardship or existential *angst*, the omission of such experience from contemporary hymnology and the over-riding emphasis on triumphalism merely serve to exacerbate their feelings of dissonance. It is wonderful for the many to sing lyrics such as 'Everybody's singing now, 'cos we're so happy, untold angels celebrate, 'cos joy is in this place'—but what about people who are suffering from depression, or who have been recently bereaved? (There are likely to be more in your congregation than you'd like to admit.) Should they pretend to be happy and deny their true feelings, or stand out like the proverbial sore thumb?

It is at best alienating and at worst soul-destroying for people to have to listen to or be encouraged to sing along to music with which they have little connection. Let's remember that spirituality does not involve some easily won feel-good factor. It is something to be worked on—in the case of music, it takes work to listen to and respond to great works—and something to move us at both our times of elation and our times of desolation. Some of the greatest pieces of music, of course, including church music, have been inspired by sadness and alienation.

To attempt to engage with people musically is an essential part of ensuring their active participation in worship and to stop them disengaging with the Church. However, when our culture is becoming so fragmented and diverse, this does creates practical problems.

Music brings to the fore this key sociological, theological and ecclesiological debate. Should the Church cater for such a fragmenting society by providing a plurality of expressions of localized (both geographically and culturally) worship, or should it try to buck the trend by promoting music within worship that attempts to unite people across the divides of age, class and musical genres?

This is a question that, until recently, would not have been an issue. In the days when culture was much more homogenous, church music often led the way. Some of the world's greatest pieces of classical music were inspired by the Bible or written for use in church. Even coming further up to date, early rock and roll was partly inspired by the sound of the black gospel choirs of the deep south of the United States. But today, in an age when culture is fragmenting at every point, and there are many different musical genres which help to define young people's identity, can we really hope to please all comers with our worship? And if so, what musical style should we adopt?

There is no definitive answer to these questions. Certainly, there was a clear emphasis on unity in the early Church (Galatians 3:28–29) but at the same time it is highly questionable whether the equality and unity that Paul calls for should result in homogeneity. The inclusion of four very different Gospels within the canon could in itself be viewed as an encouragement of diversity.

One approach is to accept our differences and work with various expressions of worship within one community. This is the approach adopted by St Mary's in Ealing of which *Grace* are a part. The Anglican ethos and established practice lends itself well to this plurality within the one community, partly because the whole parish forms the church community. We neglect the theme of unity at our peril; but perhaps we can explore different and less divisive ways of being 'united' than looking for a homogenous musical style. (The thorny issue of youth church is too complex to address in such a short book as this; but it arises from the question of the fragmentation of culture.) If we persist with unity at all costs, we run the risk of reducing everything down to a theoretically acceptable-to-all midpoint. And what are we left with? To us, it sounds like muzak or 'lift-music'.

There are a number of styles of music encompassed by churches in the UK but very few that actually bear any relation to contemporary popular culture. We personally believe that this is a contributory factor in the huge decline in people aged 15–35 attending our churches today. Music that engages people and inspires them is more likely to provide serious points of contact beyond the service. While our parents might be quite genuinely inspired by listening to guitar-based choruses that reflect the Simon and Garfunkel-style music of their choice, the chances are that the twenty-something son of their neighbour, whose drum 'n' bass reverberates through the walls, would remain unimpressed. That same twenty-something might find that the music on offer at *Grace* communicates the Christian message to him much more effectively.

Although many alternative services tend to use electronic music (many have sprung from within club culture, which revolves around dance music), that is not to say that any one style is better or worse. In fact, part of our frustration with church worship lies not with the fact that choruses are corny (although they often are—and corny music is *not* an aid to worship), but that only one style is ever represented. This is not only frustrating for those of us who tend not to respond so well to up-tempo sing-alongs; but it shows a categoric lack of creativity in, as we said, one of the most spiritual and emotive of art forms. The Church should be leading the way in its creative use of music—not, as has happened already, becoming a laughing stock for its terrible Christian bands and its lack of imagination. There are so many forms of music—from Gregorian chant to folk, and from classical to jazz—to be explored. All it takes is some musical vision.

Some people have told us they would come to services such as the Labyrinth and *Grace* even if it were just to listen to the music and relax. The use of such music in a worship context can be an incredibly powerful and liberating message to those whose perception of church is that it means leaving your cultural identity at the door. It sends a clear message that God is not intrinsically connected with just one cultural package that the worshipper must submit to in order to participate. It does not impose an identity on the outsider, but rather seeks to affirm their own identity and celebrate the richness and diversity of human experience.

Our intention is not to be prescriptive, but rather to give some idea of the ways in which alternative worship groups have used music differently from most churches. Many have made good use of low-tempo dance music, known as 'ambient', 'chill-out', 'acid-jazz' and so on. Such 'electronic' music makes an excellent backdrop and is good for talking, praying or reading over. This style of music may not be appropriate to your congregation; however, it may be that there are those within your community who would feel at home with something different from the style you currently use.

Electronic music is particularly appropriate to the postmodern worship context in that it works not by the use of a complicated lyric (much dance music has no lyrics at all) but rather by creating an atmosphere, a mood, whether that be ambient, reflective or invigorating. This is important. We have spoken about the power of words and pictures when they are allowed to stand alone, when they are left unexplained, for worshippers to respond to subjectively. Music is no different. As one of the most powerful of art forms, a piece of music without lyric and without explanation— whether it be from Olivier Messiaen to Leftfield's latest album— can touch the spirit in an inexplicable way.

As such, it can be used particularly effectively in a worship context to complement a particular element in a service. For example, you could choose your own piece to create an atmosphere suitable for a meditation on Jesus' time in the desert.

Creativity

Another key area is the importance of releasing creativity from within your own congregation. While 'off the peg' worship music has been helpful to many congregations, it can tend to stifle the emergence of new music from within.

It is all too easy to decide not to attempt any new music on the grounds that you don't have the capability to pull it off. But you can start by encouraging the musically gifted among your congregation to begin to create their own worship material, rather than waiting for the latest *Spring Harvest* tape to hit the shelves. This may include writing lyrics or composing melodies or tracks. The alternative worship groups we have been involved with have developed a wide range of music, some of which is now more widely available. It is worth remembering that the creative process is positive in and of itself. That means, it is far better to develop something slightly less polished if it releases creativity from within your worshipping community. It is then more authentic and reflects more truly the style and concerns of the wider community in your area. Don't consciously set out to ape Matt Redman or Graham Kendrick or anyone else—there is nothing more sacred about their music than yours (and they'd be the first to say so).

Worship is communion with God. Therefore the concerns should be similar to prayer, and it is helpful to blur the boundaries between prayer and worship. Worship is a space for us to be healed and to adore our Creator and the work of the Creator's 'hands'. While we would want to deconstruct the notion that a 'time of worship' is only the time when we play music or sing songs, we would also want to question the idea that we only 'worship' when we are vigorously singing songs or hymns.

The composer James MacMillan, himself a Christian, has compared helpfully the role of music and prayer:

Prayer does change us. Our convictions, our activities, our perspectives on our fellow humans, the nature of life, the nature of God, can be radically altered through giving up time to prayer. And it is the same with music. I think our perspectives are fundamentally changed through the power of music. There is an analogy there, and I think it is because they are from the same source: we are talking about the same thing.[13]

We usually think about worship in the context of praising God—it is liberating to stop and listen as an act of prayer and worship.

In alternative worship groups, there are a number of ways in which music has been typically been used. First, as a background to create an atmosphere or mood for any given context—for example, with voiceovers and meditations. At *LOPE*, most of our services took place to a quiet back-beat. This helps to create a more relaxed atmosphere and seems for most people to facilitate heightened and extended concentration on sections which involved listening to people talking.

Then, you can use music as a background for a chant or simple chorus. *Grace* makes good use of this, playing a repeatable piece of music that can be sung over. The *Grace* CDs (see the Appendix of Resources) include such pieces. This kind of simple, repeatable material can be created either by a band or more typically 'sampled' from an instrumental CD of ambient electronic music.

You can also highlight a particularly 'spiritual' lyric in a song, or use a song that illustrates a specific point. Many contemporary dance tracks make use of samples or lyrics from classic gospel music (Moby's latest album, *Play*, explicitly draws on such influences, for example) and these can be illustrated before being played and used in a worship context. At *LOPE* we often used to 'subvert' songs that our young people would be listening to on a regular basis outside church. One hauntingly evocative song, 'Protection', by Tracey Thorne of the group Everything But the Girl, included the lyric, 'I stand in front of you, I take the force of the blows... Protection'. We used this song, with its inference of pacifist intervention, to illustrate a service on sacrifice—both Christ's sacrifice for us and as an example of the need for us to stand up for justice and intervene for the powerless, locally and globally. Music can also, of course, provide a powerful accompaniment to visual images.

In all this, we remember that when it is used sensitively, music can help liberate our creativity and allow those who may not otherwise darken the door of our churches to, at the very least, try them out. At best, they will begin to worship their Creator from within a more authentic cultural setting, which can only be a wonderful thing. It is worth closing with another word from the inspirational James MacMillan.

Sounds have deeper resonances in our minds, in our psychology, in our corporeality, in our sensual selves. There is a deep connectedness between music and what it means to be human, and so music is not a remote, abstract thing. It does encapsulate something of the narrative of human life. It's not real storytelling, but it has its own drama which somehow, sometimes, reflects the real drama of everyday life and of our history.[14]

SIX

Phoning home

How on earth can you get people to pray 'alternatively'?

Prayer is a truly global activity and an integral part of any spirituality. Surveys tell us that the vast majority of the population pray at some point in their lives (some regularly), including many who never normally darken the doors of our traditional churches. There is something intrinsic in us as humans that drives us to reach out to the unknown, the transcendent, the divine. Most of us can agree, from our own experience of life, with the writer of Ecclesiastes, who said that God has set eternity in our hearts (Ecclesiastes 3:11). Whether in quiet times of despair or moments of panic, people naturally reach out to something beyond themselves. We long to communicate with God, to find 'guidance from above', to receive help in times of crisis from someone or something supremely powerful—a 'bridge over troubled waters'. Whatever theoretical and theological problems people may have in believing, their gut instinct seems to be to cry out—we believe, as Christians—to God.

If this is the case, then why do so many of these praying people ignore or avoid the Church, or the services we provide? We can, of course, talk about all sorts of issues from relevance to relativism. But when specifically it comes to prayer, perhaps part of the problem is that we ask people to fit our mould when they 'pray' in church. This is a shame—as one of the key roles of the Church must be to help facilitate an *authentic* spirituality for the people of the twenty-first century.

So, what is prayer? For Gotthold Ephraim Lessing, 'a single grateful thought raised to heaven is the most perfect prayer'. We all have our own feelings on how we should define the act, but its essence is communication with the divine. It is about voicing our needs and concerns, our sorrow and repentance. And it is about listening and contemplating, hearing the silence, waiting for the still, small voice of God to speak. It can involve getting in tune with ourselves—quiet, contemplative meditation on our lives in the light of God. Prayer can also be part of the process of letting go, of shedding or handing over the concerns of our ever-busier days.

However we define it, the Bible certainly commands us to do it, and do it often. This chapter is concerned less with personal and private devotions than with how we manage corporate prayer; but regardless of which aspect of prayer we are looking at, we must always bear in mind the significance the Bible places on the act throughout its pages. In this light, and given such a wonderful breadth of expectation, it seems strange that the way we 'do' it is so narrow, especially within our services. We often focus almost exclusively on 'cataphatic discourse': that is, us speaking out our prayers, either literally or by praying in our heads. Often prayers are communal or liturgical, led by one person from the front. And this rightly forms an integral part of corporate Christian worship. But to *restrict* ourselves to this is to deny the full range of expression and communication that we have at our disposal.

It is easy to let our prayers become almost entirely formal, 'left-brain' activities, while the instinctive, intuitive right-side of our brains is neglected. One consequence of this is that we restrict the use of our bodies in prayer. It may never have crossed our minds to be physical in our prayers—after all, we usually see it as a mind thing, closing our eyes and putting our hands together in order to shut out the physical world from our 'spiritual' thoughts. In Romans 8:26, Paul writes that 'the Spirit helps us in our weakness. We do not know what we ought to pray for, but the Spirit himself intercedes for us with groans that words cannot express.' Imagine praying with your entire body, engaging with your full emotions in what you are communicating. The modern age has left a legacy within evangelicalism of pray-ers who ensure their prayers are theologically sound, thought through and hermetically sealed; rather than prayers from the gut, the kind that Jesus offered in the garden of Gethsamene or when he wept over Jerusalem and for Lazarus.

A holistic use of prayer in worship could encompass our full emotions, involve our whole body and our whole brain. It could, primarily, allow God to speak to us. It could permit silence and contemplation, and the space to let go, to hand over our burdens and busyness. It could captivate our imaginations, and incorporate non-verbal communication. It could be open and accessible to all, including outsiders; and it could be both communal and utterly personal.

Many creative worship groups have used meditations extensively as a focus for imaginative or contemplative prayer. Two main areas seem to be commonly used. The first involves taking people on a journey of the mind. The person who is leading the meditation might typically read out a series of prompts or instructions which enable those taking part to explore their imaginations, or to consider an 'issue' or perhaps something in the news from a spiritual perspective. You might, for example, be encouraged to imagine being part of a story in the Bible, to explore what the situation might have really felt like, what the sights and smells were, what characters were involved, how you might have felt... Imagine, for instance, being one of those people who were waiting to stone the woman caught in adultery (John 8). Imagine that you are holding a stone. How big is it? Feel its texture. You can see the woman, you can feel the emotion, you can sense the kill. Look her in the eye. What do you see? Terror? Confusion? Regret? Look around you. What are others saying? Are there children present? Feel the sun beating down on you. You might imagine an encounter with Jesus. What might you say to him after he has uttered those terrible words, 'Let him who is without sin among you be the first to throw a stone at her'? (*Step Into the Light*, published by BRF, is just such a collection of Bible-based meditations, ready for use—see the Appendix of Resources.)

This kind of imaginative journey can inspire and engage your congregation far more intensively than a simple reading of a passage might do, and it can form a vivid and creative part of your corporate prayer life. It can help you to become part of the action, to allow the reality and historicity of the situation to seep through you. Our treatment of Bible passages can so often remove the earthiness of God's encounter with real human beings; it can lessen the power of the story, and reduce the real, three-dimensional characters of the action into cardboard cutouts of the mind. To bring those characters back to life is to involve yourself creatively with the story of God, to allow God to communicate again with you through his story, to meditate on the message—to pray.

Or, you might simply offer a time of contemplation. For example, you could encourage a period of silence after reading a Bible story or a passage or just get people to think about a theme. This sounds so simple: but 'alternative' worship need not be complicated or technological. Silence and space have become rare commodities in our fast-forward, consumer culture. It is vital that we make room for quiet. It could be the only point in the week that busy people actually get the time to stop and think—about themselves, each other, God, our place as created beings within creation. You might use a short prayer—for example, 'The Lord is my God: in him I trust'—which can be spoken or sung repeatedly by the group. This kind of response also helps people pray on a less cerebral level—that is, they can respond with their hearts. And they may wish to lie on the floor or find a more comfortable position. Sitting upright in a pew might not always be most conducive to allowing our imaginations to flourish.

You might encourage your congregation to participate in a silent 'letting go' meditation which precedes a longer time of corporate prayer. When we come to the business of prayer, we usually enter it with our minds and bodies full of the stresses of the day. We can and should bring these to God: apart from the practical fact that otherwise you are likely to dwell on them and thus miss a profound encounter with God, this does, in fact, help us to acknowledge that God is all about the stuff of life, involved in our everyday actions and feelings.

Often, people can find themselves being manipulated in church to 'project' an image of themselves to the others around them. In one church we visited, the leadership team—which sat on the front row—turned around during the time of singing in order to watch people's faces. This was intimidating, and made us feel obliged to smile and look joyful. It is quite an extreme example, but it can happen in much milder—yet still manipulative—ways. It is a fine line between exhorting your congregation to 'be joyful in the Lord' and making them become people they are not. A teacher whose life has been made hell all week may well feel that they have to maintain a positive tone and impression, whether they feel like it or not. Instead, in times of quiet meditation, you can encourage people to face their feelings—be true to themselves and each other—and communicate with God about how they feel and who they are.

Such a meditation might even incorporate some relaxation exercises, such as controlled breathing and the tensing and relaxing of muscles (which is perhaps best achieved lying down). It may also be helpful to do something physical to help people enact the process of 'setting down' or letting go their concerns. One popular way is to ask your congregation to write on a piece of paper their main worries. You can then pass around a bin in which these worries can then be symbolically placed, or even burnt. This does not mean that people should be encouraged to deny the negative aspects of their life—it means that these concerns should be embraced and faced up to—but it helps to demonstrate symbolically that we can indeed 'cast our burdens upon Jesus'.

The Labyrinth is a good example of a 'walking meditation' that involves many of the elements we mention above. As we explained in the Introduction, it derives from an ancient form of spiritual 'exercise'. It was typically walked by those preparing for baptism or Easter time, but it serves very effectively as a more regular discipline. The Labyrinth is truly multi-faceted, offering many layers of meaning and numerous metaphorical connections with the Christian pilgrim in their life-journey. Ideally it is walked very slowly; and as you walk, you slow your breathing and begin to follow the path. It incorporates three stages: the inward section, in which you are encouraged to envisage a journey towards God; the central area, which symbolizes communion with God; and the outward path, during which the pilgrim ventures back out into the 'world', taking with them the confidence of their experience with God.

The Labyrinth reflects a number of themes. On the inward journey you are encouraged to let go or shed those things which hinder and hold you back from a relationship with God. This might include sinful actions or patterns of behaviour, or the clutter and hassle of everyday life that seems to stifle both your imagination and spiritual journey. Or it might involve beginning to deal with personal pretence and allowing the authentic you, 'the you of you' as the author Douglas Coupland once put it, to surface.[15] Throughout the Labyrinth, the concept of journey is uppermost.

Such an idea strikes a chord with the contemporary reinstatement of the understanding of conversion *as a process*—one that is punctuated by moments of joy and crisis—not simply a one-off, be-all-and-end-all commitment. The theme of spiritual or faith journey within missiology is becoming more readily embraced, and the Labyrinth reflects this—along with the idea that we are all continuing to search after God, and that we may not have arrived. Thus the 'Christians' and those who would not describe themselves as such can walk the Labyrinth alongside one another; it is accessible to all who are on a journey. It could, if used well, help to deconstruct our separatism and make prayer accessible to the 70 or 80 per cent of the population who pray but do not attend church and are variously described as 'non-Christians', 'not-yet-Christians', 'agnostics' and so on. It may mean that we need to let go of our eagerness to score a conversion, as they say in rugby. And it may mean that we need to become less hasty to find out whether people are 'really' Christians, and more ready to allow people to be themselves, where they are 'at' spiritually, in order to allow them to begin to walk the Christian path. If this were to happen, we might see many more people coming into our churches, and looking, we would like to think, in the right places for their holy grail.

The Labyrinth is a wonderful example (and a physical demonstration) of how prayer can be both corporate and individual at the same time—people walk individually, yet everyone is involved. It can encourage honesty in prayer, and can help us to think about becoming more authentically human along our journey. It can incorporate less obvious 'Christians' and allow for safe, inspiring and authentic spiritual exploration. And it can transform lives—by helping pilgrims to enact their walk with God visually, and physically and spiritually move closer to the divine.

Another radically simple but remarkably effective idea we used from time to time at *Live On Planet Earth* is the 'prayer tree'. You can collect a fallen branch and, during the service, invite people to come and write a prayer on a small strip of paper, which they can then stick on to the wood. As more and more add their prayers to it, the tree begins to take shape, each prayer representing a single leaf. The effect is visually very stimulating (not to say moving), and collects the individual prayers of the group together in one place as a corporate offering to God. For those who prefer to express their prayers in a different way, you can encourage painting or drawing, perhaps, or the modelling of clay. The collections of visible, artistic expressions of prayer that we have seen have been truly inspirational. They stand as a testament to the creativity of people who are communicating with the divine; and they show work, effort, thought, imagination. So often, we see prayer as something easy or throwaway. But it takes effort, sometimes, to keep relationships fresh. And such imaginative exploration is both rewarding and pleasing, surely, to God. The end result can be a corporate prayer, demonstrating the individuality—yet the connectedness—of the group.

We have also made much use of candles in our services. Candles are loaded with Christian tradition and symbolism, and they help to create an evocative setting which doesn't have to be reserved for the Christmas carol service. Neither does the lighting of candles to accompany prayers need to be exclusive to the Catholic tradition. Such an act helps to imbue your prayer with a sense of significance and occasion. We know that the immanence of our new covenant God means that we don't *have* to light candles for God to notice our prayers, but as we've already stated, the style in which we do our worship is important and can help enormously to release the huge potential of a deeper spirituality.

Psalm 141:2 and Revelation 8:3–4 invoke the metaphorical notion that our prayers are like the smoke of incense rising into God's nostrils. We have loved using incense in our services because of this symbolic significance; and again because it creates a real sense of prayerfulness, of anticipation of an encounter with God. It helps emphasize the point that this is an occasion of importance, of holiness. As with candles, the use of incense has been largely confined to the Orthodox, High Anglican and Catholic traditions. As evangelicals we have become suspicious of such tools of worship, often denouncing them as 'New Age' or worse. They should hold no fears; though neither should you use them just because most alternative worship groups do so. Try it and see if those within your group find it a useful aid to contemplation and prayer. (One word of caution: if you use incense or joss sticks, be aware of the potential danger to asthmatics.)

If we are serious about rediscovering our spiritual depth—about taking time, and using our creativity, to explore more fully the sense of awe and wonder which should naturally accompany an experience of God—then we can unlock a host of ways and means that will take us closer to this end. It is not that we have done things wrongly in the past, but we can take this opportunity, as society yearns for a sense of the spiritual as it drowns in the mire of the material, to demonstrate that as Christians we are made in the image of a wonderful Creator God, who has set in us the longing and the capacity to commune with the divine.

SEVEN

Clashing symbols

We have already explored in some detail the contemporary cultural resistance to claims of 'objectivity'. And we have seen how Christian worship that acknowledges and incorporates a less dogmatic and more subjective approach can help to provide a more accessible church 'experience'. This principle is perhaps especially borne out when it comes to symbolism.

The Protestant tradition has been wary of anything vaguely pictorial or symbolic ever since the Reformers split from the Church over a series of complex and interwoven political and theological issues in the sixteenth century. It is hard to separate the politics from the theology around this traumatic time (and in some places, such as Northern Ireland, the divide between religion and politics is still hard to distinguish). Catholic practices had, to an extent, become over-religious—to the point, for example, where it was *icons* of Jesus that many were worshipping, and not Jesus himself. But there is a danger, as with any revolution, of throwing the baby out with the bathwater. Icons and symbols and pictures were useful, for example, to the many illiterate 'commoners' in the days before the printing press, when they were otherwise reliant on their priest to explain to them the scriptures. Today, they may be useful to the spiritually illiterate, of whom there are many. Icons and symbols once allowed space for visual creativity, contemplation and spirituality—which we have now, to a large extent, not only lost, but become hostile towards. Yet a healthy degree of symbolism, of ritual, of the visual demonstration of our Christian spirituality, is crucial, especially in a culture which has grown up watching images rather than reading books.

As Western culture now moves away from the predilections of the Enlightenment, we are left with an excellent and exciting opportunity to reclaim elements of our 'traditional' Christian heritage which we jettisoned with the Reformation. Just as New Age searchers might 'pick and mix' their own spiritualities, there is no reason why we should not begin to plunder our wonderfully rich Christian heritage in order to create a deeper Christian spirituality for the new century. Many of the elements of worship that worked in premodern culture might be just as effective in this postmodern time.

It is fair to say that there has been a blurring of the edges in terms of icons and images among many creative worship groups. Icons do have a more fixed set of meanings than images or other symbols, but they still embody the notion that worship can occur through the use of physical objects that connect the worshipper with the divine, without becoming objects of worship themselves. While many groups do not use icons in their traditional sense (though some do), most have taken their prompt from the traditional use of icons in Christian worship to 'play' with the idea of images and symbols as a vital component of worship in the postmodern context.

We believe it is essential for the Western (Protestant) Church to recognize and revisit some of these ancient traditions and to embrace more positively aspects of Orthodoxy as well as Catholicism. Simon Jenkins' excellent introduction to the use and tradition of icons in Orthodoxy, *Windows into Heaven*,[16] explores how the Eastern Church has done much thinking about how to use words and images within worship. Icons have perhaps been explored less by alternative worship groups; but symbolism— from the lighting of candles to the recontextualizing of the Eucharist[17]—has been widely embraced. The Labyrinth, as we have seen, was a 'symbol' that was adopted and 'Christianized' by the medieval church. Many alternative worship groups have found that a wide range of people, from curious enquirers—including those from other faiths—to devout believers, respond very positively and enthusiastically to its layers of symbolism in the present day.

Perhaps the key is the way in which such ancient symbols are reworked or re-appropriated for present cultures. It is the creative fusion of ancient tradition with contemporary culture that can bring about exciting new possibilities. It has been exciting, for example, to take the original theme of the inward journey of the Labyrinth—that of 'shedding', or 'letting go'—and recontextualizing it through various symbolic acts for the twenty-first century, for a consumer culture in which the issue of personal identity has become so important and so confusing to so many. The process of letting go allows us to think again, within the context of worship, about the multiple layers of our identities. Which are projections, which are simply false, and which really help to comprise our core?

Many Christians' concerns about symbolism and icons have arisen from a mixture of misunderstanding and a lingering anti-Catholicism. Critics of the use of icons and symbols in worship allege idolatry, suggesting that the icon becomes the object of worship itself. Certainly, it is important to retain the distinction between the sign and the signifier—that is, between the icon and that to which it points. The value of an icon or a symbol lies in the way it brings a tangible quality to our relationship with God.

Concerns over the icon becoming itself an object of worship emerge from a misunderstanding of the true nature of metaphor. The Orthodox tradition does not expect or encourage people to view icons as things to be worshipped in and of themselves, and neither are icons seen as an exact replica of the person or situation depicted. Such an idea springs from modernism's preoccupation with objectivity, and would not have been an important issue in the original roots of iconography.

We have referred, earlier, to the place of metaphor within creative worship. As we seek to apply parallels and encourage a connection between the mundane and the divine, metaphor plays a key role. It is vital that we understand the prominence and significance of metaphor to religion and the appropriate use of symbolism and symbolic acts. Born in the era when the Church was trying to re-establish Christianity in the face of the perceived threat from the Enlightenment and modernity (with its scientific discoveries and emphasis on rationalism and reason), evangelicalism has tended to play down the role and place of metaphor within worship. The methods used to combat the challenges posed by modernity and the Enlightenment were to a large extent modernist and rationalist. People were asking whether Christianity was really true—so apologetics were an ideal way of answering their questions. Evangelicalism used modernist methods to interact with the people of modernity (much as creative worship groups are trying to do with the emerging postmodern worldview). But perhaps in doing so, evangelicalism has actually tied itself too tightly to the trappings of modernism and has become entrenched in a modernist worldview. Meanwhile, the world has moved on and people are asking different questions.

Metaphor does not fit so easily with the rational, modernist mindset because it is not, in itself, empirical, literal and objective. Colin Gunton, in discussing the cross as a metaphor, laments the fact that 'the view of metaphor as an abuse of language came, like other rationalist beliefs, to its climax in the Age of Reason... Metaphor is disqualified from being a means of our rational interaction with the world: *unless it ceases to be metaphor, it cannot tell the truth.*'[18] Yet its very claim to subjectivity—it demands interaction from whoever encounters it—means that its place within worship can help to provide a vital link for spiritual searchers in the quest for the divine amid everyday culture.

Dave Tomlinson, in his book *The Post-Evangelical*,[19] provides an excellent summary of the value and place of metaphor, both within the faith and within postmodern society. He suggests:

A great deal hinges on the sort of understanding we have of metaphor. Historically metaphors have been understood as figures of speech, or colourful ways of saying something which could easily be put more plainly. Nowadays, we recognize the situation to be rather more complicated than this; we now know that metaphors are an essential part of the way we grasp reality; in other words, they yield real information, which cannot necessarily be gained or understood in any other way.

Metaphor is thus an important tool within the range of elements we have in our worship. People appreciate the honesty that comes from acknowledging that our own attempts and those of the Bible to connect the mundane and the divine are constrained by the tension between the 'is' and the 'is not' of its subject. Jesus uses a variety of metaphors to describe God: he refers to God as 'father', and yet God is not literally a father as we understand one. The Father did not exist before the Son; and God the Father does not have a gender, nor was he involved in the procreation of the Son. God's attributes are *metaphorically* like those of a good father towards his child.

Wisdom is needed in the use of metaphor. Some of the young people we worked with had father figures who were unreliable, absent, neglectful and so on—which is not a very positive description of what God might be like. The recurring theme of 'God as Father' in many contemporary worship choruses was therefore not that helpful in conveying the true nature of God. So we took time in our worship to explain that any metaphorical references to God that we might make were just that: metaphors, not literal descriptions. There are ways in which God 'is' and 'is not' like a father. This neither undermines nor detracts from the metaphor; in fact it enhances it. The metaphor is freed up to be what it was intended to be, and is no longer constrained by the shackles of literalism.

We also took time to balance such perspectives, as did Jesus, by underlining the (stereo)typically feminine attributes and aspects of God's character and nature. This provided a useful balance to people's perceptions that the Church and the Bible are patriarchal and misogynist, in contrast to the emphasis on equality within wider culture.

A vital element of the Christian faith is the need for a relationship with Jesus and God, and yet little attention is paid to the difficulties that this idea presents. Our human understanding of relationship is of something that constitutes ongoing, two-way communication; and yet for many (or most) Christians, the reality is that their relationship with Jesus is intangible and bears little resemblance to a normal one. We scrape the proverbial barrel for the merest hint of a response or a reply. When people tell us that 'God told me to do such and such a thing', we rarely push for an explanation of what this actually means because we know it will mean nothing more than that 'I felt this is what I should do' or that 'something came into my mind'. 'Relationship' can become little more than a transcendental or psychological exercise, and worship can easily become an extension of this.

Many people are sceptical about a religion that takes such subjective 'encounters' and constructs objective truth-claims around them. Jonny Baker has pointed out that alternative worship groups, with their emphasis on an incarnational theology, tend to recognize and acknowledge that all encounters with the divine are *mediated*. '[An incarnational approach] doesn't need to make such great claims for its take on the story or the experiences people have. It attempts to improvise faithfully to "enable people to encounter God within the context of their own subcultural sign/symbol posts" but recognizes the planner's part in the construction.'[20]

Host of symbols

Jesus was an active participant in Jewish worship, which was steeped in symbolism and acts of remembrance, feasts and so on. And he certainly understood and built upon the symbolism of his religion. Indeed, the most powerful and enduring of Christian symbolic acts is Jesus' recapitulation of the Passover feast within the Eucharist. When Jesus left the disciples, he left perhaps the most significant symbolic act by which we might remember him. (And certainly one of the most contentious: much of the thinking of the Reformers hinged around whether or not the 'elements' really became transubstantiated—that is, whether they literally became the body and blood of Christ once they were consecrated.) He did not leave us with a purely transcendental relationship—he left us with the mysterious reality of bread and wine.

The Eucharist is a symbolic act that works subjectively with each participant, and powerfully with 'the many'. The fact that Jesus initiated it as a primary act of remembrance and worship means we can safely assume that symbolic acts could, and probably should, play a very significant part in our acts of worship.

The Eucharist, with its bread and wine, is a potent and direct symbol; yet it should not prevent us from developing other symbolic acts which might be helpful in a contemporary context. We can search for tangible acts that help us to connect our worship with our everyday lives, the mundane with the divine. Such acts or rituals comprise a significant part of Celtic spirituality, in which a task as mundane as clearing out a fireplace could be linked to a daily life of prayer and worship. Most of us don't have real fires now; but there are mundane tasks that we do that can be linked to worship. In so doing, worship can be taken out of the service and applied to our lives. Something that triggers a deliberate inclusion of God in our everyday activities—such as starting a journey or switching on the computer—might be very helpful.

At *Grace* Jonny Baker developed a wonderful symbolic act reflecting the highs and lows of life. As preparation for the service, he bought some lemons, jars of honey and breadsticks. He explained that we all experience days and even moments that are simply 'sweet'. These are like honey, and we can easily imagine that God is with us at such times. However, it is easy to forget God when things are going well, and we should acknowledge the good times and thank God for them. We also all have periods when things turn bitter. We should remember that God is equally with us in these moments; God stands with us in our pain. Such bitter moments are like lemon.

To the strains of 'Bitter Sweet Symphony' by a band called The Verve, the congregation were encouraged to come and dip a breadstick into some honey and taste it. Then they moved on to bite into a slice of lemon, acknowledging God's presence with them in the bitter moments of life. The honey and lemon were positioned at 'stations' around the worship space. In the weeks that followed the service, people noted how easy it was to identify honey or lemon days. As such, the symbol not only provided a tangible and memorable activity but also an ongoing and helpful connection with their lives. This in turn took the worship experience beyond the constraints of the service; it projected forward and helped us to allow God into both our good and bad future experiences. Thus, in a very powerful way our worship service is enhanced and becomes more real; but our lives as a congregation are integrated more, as individual and corporate acts of worship.

In one service at *LOPE*, we explored the theme of the incarnation. We were drawing on the prologue to John's Gospel, in which the incarnation is described as 'the Word [logos] becoming flesh'. A contemporary way of describing this might be to say that in the incarnation the Christ, in Jesus, got his hands dirty—he mucked in and got involved with humanity. As a symbolic response to this and the implied exhortation for us to do likewise—to get our hands dirty and 'incarnate' the love of Christ to others around us—we devised a very simple but potent symbol. We laid out a clean white sheet on the ground and mixed up a bucket of liquid mud. The congregation was encouraged to dip their hands in the mud and place them on the sheet as a symbol of gratitude to Christ for the incarnation and of commitment on our part to do likewise. As each person in turn came forward, we produced a communal, corporate symbol of our intention to be Christ to those in our community and beyond.

Sometimes you can really push the metaphorical boat out. The next example shows how, on one level, alternative worship can easily be dismissed by some as wacky or 'dodgy'. But if you take the time to stop, look and listen, it can really provide some wonderfully creative stimulation. The service was at *Epicentre*, the creative arts group based in Battersea. And the Eucharist was rather different from your average Sunday morning service. Alex Gowing-Cumber, who had been developing a 'cyber-feminist' liturgy[21] with his wife Kat, explains:

As part of my studies at Ridley Hall, I was exploring the challenge of a eucharistic liturgy for cyber-feminists. The idea was to wrestle through some of the human struggles, both good and bad, which got people to this point, and especially the problems people had embracing Jesus in a post-Christian cyber culture. The extra point of interest was having a few Catholic women on the course and all their wrestling with issues around communion, both theologically and in terms of church power-struggles and so on. It soon became easy to see why so much baggage had got in the way of cyber-feminists getting close to Christ.

The idea went something like this: I wanted to devise a service which was in many respects allegorical but also enabled people who had either never got their heads round Christ and never received communion, or else felt totally alienated, to 'have a go'. The reading in the service was a cyber-punk allegory of the gospel based around a part-cyborg character called Jess, living in a post-nuclear Jerusalem with parents who worked for a government regime in its euthanasia development plant. Using a soundtrack including DJ rap (a female DJ), we approached communion with clips from the 1920s film Metropolis *in the background, as well as images from* Lawnmower Man. *We celebrated communion in the light* of the cyber gospel. So a computer circuit board was broken in half (expensive for weekly parish use unless you have a source of scrap parts), and the energy drink Red Bull was used to represent Christ's energy and life force.

Prior to the service people were encouraged to opt out at any point if they wanted to, but interestingly, nobody did. We weren't talking about kids, but women in their thirties and forties; and when the cup of Red Bull was passed round I was fully expecting people to abstain, but nobody did (in fact the Catholic women, who would really struggle over this issue, took 'communion', so to speak, from a lay Anglican and found it a powerful time of drawing close to Jesus in a new way).

So all of that was in our minds when spending September on a month's placement working with Epicentre. [We were also thinking about] conversations with some members who had been looking at icons and times in church history when physical affection had been shown to these. We wanted to devise a way of telling the story of the cyber-feminist gospel (issues of inclusivity being very important to Epicentre) and combining it with this new eucharistic act while dealing in a deeper way with issues of meeting with God in a way which cut through a lot of conservative attitudes about 'God: the man who tells you off'. We wanted somehow to hug God and feel God's pain at the way our distorted love crucified Jesus.

Keeping the cyber theme, we were walking down Battersea High Street when we saw a six-foot inflatable alien. Somehow, we knew this held the key. We took it home to experiment. We devised a liturgy, and, combining it with some of the experimental ideas mentioned above (and would you believe I walked past a shop replacing its security system and was able to get the circuit board out of the old one!), we came up with a plan that allowed us to embrace Christ, who in many ways was the alien. While doing so, we demonstrated both love and guilt: as the first person hugged the alien, we took the air stopper out. With each hug, *breath was squeezed out. The circle was just about big enough that, by the time the alien had got round, it was like a limp, sick body—and the final hug made a whoosh noise like a dying breath. A couple of people got very tearful.*

At the end of the service we talked about Pentecost and new life being breathed into the Church. As the earthly embodiment of Christ, we then corporately re-inflated the alien, passing it to one another like a communion chalice. When it was big again I took it and stood it by the altar, where it had been at the start of worship.

This is a very avant-garde way of celebrating the Eucharist and an extreme example of alternative worship. If you simply heard that someone had used an inflatable alien to symbolize Christ as part of a Eucharist service, you might have been rather shocked. But the point is that people like Alex and Kat, who are involved in trying to find new ways of worshipping with people outside the 'mainstream', pave the way for the rest of us to try unusual things in our services. They—like many others in alternative and creative worship groups around the country—take the risks and the flak. They dare to think differently and not to dismiss some-thing just because it doesn't automatically fit into the pre-conceived ideas of the way church should be done.

The Labyrinth service, too, is full of a huge variety of symbolic acts which encompass some wider themes of symbolism. A key one is journey. The service is a journey in itself and it refers to and symbolizes the journey of faith that each of us walks throughout our lives. The Labyrinth begins with the act of foot washing, a re-enactment of Jesus washing his disciples' feet. (Incidentally, this also takes place in some High Anglican churches on Maundy Thursday.) This act of humility emphasizes the solidarity of each and every person at the service. It symbolizes that we are all walking this journey together.

At another service we were exploring the theme of unity and

diversity. We had been listening to a reading from 1 Corinthians 12:12ff. in which Paul talks of each part of the body of Christ playing a unique and vital role. We used an idea which we stole from Pip Wilson at the Greenbelt Arts Festival, where he played the famous U2 song 'One'. We arranged everyone into groups of six to eight. As the music played and Bono sang out, 'We are one, but we're not the same. We get to carry each other... One', one person from each group lay flat on the floor, while the rest very slowly lifted them up as high as possible and then lowered them back down. This helped to emphasize and celebrate our own unique identity as individual persons within the group—yet our connectedness, the fact that we are one, but not the same. At the same time, as we physically 'carried' one another, we thought of ways in which we might metaphorically carry and hold one another in the week ahead.

As you can see from these examples, there are any number of creative ways in which symbolic acts can be devised and used in worship. Remember that they are well worth the effort that goes into dreaming them up and organizing them. The best ones are those that work on a range of different levels with different people; that are inclusive, participatory, engage a range of senses and provide points of contact and connection into our everyday lives.

EIGHT

Generating wholiness

The holistic approach—'holism'—has in the last few years been applied to a range of activities, most notably within the pastoral or caring professions. Carers have begun to realize that it is less effective to treat symptoms or problems in isolation than it is to see the wider picture and meet the needs of the 'whole' person. If a person is experiencing physical manifestations of illness, for example, they may be asked whether they are happy, at home, or at work, and so on. The role played by stress will also be explored. And people are far more open to complementary medicine—to techniques and processes that serve to heal the whole self, and not just the physical part of the body that is ailing. If someone has an eating disorder, for example, the doctor will be keen nowadays to assess what shape their overall life is in, what happened in their past, how their relationships have developed, how they see themselves, and so on. Our healing professions try to attain wholeness—physical, spiritual, mental.

This can be a useful control on and guide to our approaches to worship, and can help us to see worship in the wider context of *being* church as opposed to *doing* church. And this is very timely: we now live in a society in which more and more people experience 'multiphrenia'—that is, they feel as if they have to be different people in different situations. Many of us live divided 'lives' as we assume different personas in the different social contexts with which we now have to navigate. Some find this liberating—they enjoy the freedom of identity that comes with being able to adopt a different look or personality depending upon who they are with or which context they find themselves in. But for others, it causes distress. We often have to accommodate seemingly contradictory lifestyles and behavioural patterns, depending on who we are talking to or what is expected of us.

In an image-saturated culture, what we look like seems to determine who we actually are. We are judged on how we look, and categorized by the 'viewer' as a particular type of person. Image equals identity. And the Church 'buys' this approach, too, in determining our levels of holiness. Are we really that much of a 'rebel' because we wear an earring, or a tongue-stud, for example? Are we more respectable (and thus holy or God-fearing) if we conform to type and wear a shirt and tie, or a floral dress, to church? In the eyes of many, we are. Perhaps one crucial question we need to ask as Christians in this new century is, 'In an image-saturated culture, what does it mean to be made in the image of God?'

This becomes especially apparent when it comes to thinking about our identity as Christians. So much of our idea of holiness is caught up in trying to live an appropriate Christian lifestyle (which is usually white and middle-class) that we can actually end up feeling schizophrenic when we walk into church. Whether it is simply that we feel we have to dress in a different way or change the way we speak—or, more extreme, whether we are called to ditch our non-Christian partner because the elders tell us to— many people feel that the 'real' them is left on the coat-hook as they walk through the vestibule. This is even more saddening and maddening when you consider that, as Christians, we are called to become authentically human as we grow nearer to Christ. The need for 'wholeness' and authenticity is therefore an ecclesio-logical as well as a missiological issue. Where can we truly find ourselves, let alone *be* ourselves?

One consequence of this Christian 'schizophrenia' is the increasing difficulty it creates in engaging and interacting with the world outside the church community. The mandate to be 'in the world but not of it' (John 17:13–19) is as hard today as it has ever been. Fear of the unknown has led some of our more conservative Christian leaders and churches to encourage their congregations to shun contemporary culture and 'the world', perhaps placing too much emphasis on Paul's command, 'Do not conform any longer to the pattern of this world' (Romans 12:2). As a consequence, many Christians, particularly impressionable young people and new converts, have reacted by immersing themselves in the Christian subculture—listening to Christian music and radio stations, reading Christian books and magazines, going to Christian conferences, camps and festivals, visiting Christian websites, watching Christian cable television. All of this contributes to creating a seemingly safe pseudo-culture of our own. The biggest irony is, however, that at times this subculture can become as commercialized and manipulative as the secular world it shuns. It certainly goes against the grain of the incarnation, the example of Jesus coming to live among us. The end result of such splendid isolationism is that Christians become 'of the world but not in it'!

For people like us personally, on the fringes of the mainstream Church, these Christian cultural alternatives are little more than pale imitations of their secular counterparts. We choose not to buy into this Christian world, yet we remain Christians. This creates a tremendous tension and pressure, resulting in our living 'dualistic lives'; that is, being one person when living in our church world and another in the rest of our lives. The culture within which we feel more at home is viewed as an anathema by many parts of the Church and it is not reflected in most mainstream Christian worship, and so our lives become more fragmented and less 'whole'. It is incredibly difficult to feel that you are being authentic if you don't buy into the Christian subculture, and many people who haven't had the 'alternatives' we've had, such as *Live On Planet Earth* and *Grace*, either live utterly fragmented lives or they simply walk away—both from church and their Christian faith.

It may be presumptuous to speak on behalf of the many thousands who have abandoned the Church in the last twenty years but, knowing plenty who have voted with their feet, we believe we are at least as qualified as the next person to offer some insights. The tension that arises from separatist theologies does much to drive people in their twenties and thirties, the so-called Generation X, away from the Church. At best, it says nothing to them about their lives. At worst, it asks them to become someone they are not. While we would resist the 'easy to swallow' consumerist approach to spirituality offered by the New Age, the fact that its attempts to connect with the divine also connect so tangibly with contemporary culture and lifestyles is a lesson the Church could do well to heed. Although the New Age has an overemphasis on personal fulfilment (without the outward perspective of the Christian mandate to 'love thy neighbour'), nevertheless, its emphasis on individual wholeness has not struck a chord with society without reason. (For a very helpful overview of the New Age and what we can learn from it, try reading John Drane's book, *Evangelism for a New Age*.[22])

It is also a sad fact that many new Christians quickly lose track of their 'non-Christian' friends as they get lost in a world of homegroups, revival meetings and so on. The problem with this is that, far from making the most of an all-too-rare point of contact with the outside world, the church assimilates the new convert into its 'other' world. Growing up as young adults in our local church, we were told by our youth group leaders that we shouldn't listen to secular music or go to the pub. Yet these were the two main ways that young people relaxed in country villages where there were no cinema, no bowling alleys and certainly no Christian cafés. They were effectively asking us to cut our contacts with our friends—and deny our own culture and upbringing. Contemporary missionary movements would be appalled at such cultural imperialism by the Church, if this were done abroad.

A friend of ours was keen on clubbing, and he used to attend raves across the country with a tight-knit group of friends. His family were members of the local Baptist church and he had experienced a church upbringing, but had rejected it in his teens for his alternative community of clubbers. He then experienced an encounter with Christ and started coming back to church, but all too soon he was subjected to a subtle but persistent pressure to ditch his clubbing friends because they took drugs (he had never been into this part of the scene anyway, and had become a total abstainer).

While this pressure may have been placed on him for reasons which were valid in the minds of the church leaders, such a move would not only have alienated this young man from his friends, but it would have communicated a message that they and their culture are not acceptable to the Church and consequently to God. In contrast, we tried to encourage him to maintain contacts and to continue to go out with his friends from time to time, but there was an undeniable tension within him. He became our DJ at *LOPE* and took an active part in revitalizing the music we played. As a direct result of his clubbing subculture, he brought fresh insights into ways of relating to other people in the team that were a lesson to us regarding the nature of community.

This is a messy and unresolved example. However, it serves to underline the differences that can arise from a holistic approach, which openly seeks to find common ground, unite with and learn from other cultures, as opposed to a dualistic, two-worlds approach in which people either cut links with or, more inevitably, keep separate their Christian and non-Christian worlds. If we try to employ the former method, we might find ways in which church could become a lot more accessible, especially to those social groups who typically never come along. The point is that it's OK and actually a very positive thing for Christians to have friends outside the church, and that these friendship groups should not just be seen as potential converts.

For many people who are likely to go out partying or clubbing on a Saturday night and would not be asleep before 3am, the Sunday morning service would be a distinct problem. The obvious move is a service targeted at these people in the evening or, better still, mid-week. But how many churches would countenance such a concession to the prevailing culture of twenty-somethings? (However, we probably *would* run an Alpha course at the most efficacious time, which reveals another dualism in our thinking—that between mission and worship. Some churches are willing to show the utmost flexibility when it comes to mission, but are slower to incorporate cultural sensitivity to the structure of their 'worship' times. The expectation is that once people have joined our club, they must play by our rules.) If we are serious about allowing these people an opportunity to worship God then we will remove as many obstacles as possible without compromising our faith. Lord Runcie once stated that '[we should accept] the culture is against us; and accept a drop in numbers'.[23] But we can choose not to assume such a negative approach, and, in the process, we might ourselves learn fresh ways of worshipping God.

The desire for wholeness has been one of the driving forces behind many creative worship groups. In a magazine article, a spokesperson for *Grace* said, 'The major motivation [in setting up the group] had been dissatisfaction, an increasing frustration at church culture which played music we'd never listen to at home and used language we wouldn't use anywhere else.'[24] As young people, to be told by our respected Christian leaders to bin (or even burn) our 'secular' music indiscriminately tore us apart. The fact that this still goes on in some mainstream churches is a sad indictment of our lack of ability to engage in a constructive critique of contemporary culture. Surely, a more positive approach is to encourage people of all ages to assess what they can affirm and what they would criticize of any manifestation of contemporary culture, be that television, film, music or art. We can then counter culture—which, of course we are called to do—much more effectively at the critical points.

One way we can stand out as 'salt and light' in our world is by trying to live lives that are 'whole' and providing churches and Christian worship which encourage others to do the same. The consequence of this is that our worship should reflect more closely our lives outside church and vice versa. Keith Green once wrote a song in which he prayed that his whole life would be a prayer to God: 'Make my life a prayer to you, I wanna do what you want me to do. No empty words and no white lies, no token prayers, no compromise.' We need to help people to rediscover, especially in today's culture of split and fragmented personalities, authentic human identity. We have, as Christians, the very best model of identity to draw on—that of the Trinity. It is comprised of individual 'persons' whose individuality is celebrated; yet its members form a perfect community, too. At its best, our worship actually starts to remedy our multiphrenic malaise and helps us to connect our real selves to God—and to experience a new level of communion with, and identity, as human beings. The symbolic act involving honey and lemon described in the previous chapter does just this, as the connection with everyday life is made and the worship experience is taken out into the rest of our lives.

Many alternative worship groups are concerned to create worship that is not just about our minds but engages the whole of our person, including our physical bodies as well. We are keen to do away with dualisms that elevate the mind over against the body. Such Platonic dualism has infiltrated Christian attitudes more than we might imagine. At worst the Christian faith becomes reduced to a series of cerebral 'decisions', with the elite Christians being those academics who can philosophize with the best of them. We are not advocating dumbing down the Christian faith or discouraging people from thinking about their beliefs—far from it!—but we should be wary of the tendency to limit Christianity to rationalism.

So often, our worship primarily engages only the left-hand side of our brains, which is primarily concerned with the rational and systematic, the bit we use when totting up our bank statements. We too often neglect the right side, that which creates the uncontrollable welling-up inside when we view the breathtaking beauty of the world from the top of a snow-covered mountain with friends, or when we are beside the deathbed of a loved one. In order to live fulfilled lives, we need to engage our whole brain by loving and laughing and weeping, as well as contemplating, assessing and critiquing. So also we need to engage the whole of our brains and bodies in worship. The worship of our Creator should not be a dull, uninspiring, one-dimensional experience; it should be exciting, inspiring, awesome and multi-dimensional. It should incorporate the physical, the spiritual and the psychological.

Practically speaking, it is possible to incorporate a range of sensory experiences within worship. In one service, we asked people to walk over a tray of stones, barefoot; followed by a length of cottonwool. So often we are cut off from the natural world by our surroundings; we experience less and less what it means to be a part of creation, a part of the cycle of seasons. We can buy strawberries every month of the year in the supermarket, for example. We don't need to wait until June. And so we forget that it takes warmth and light to grow them. By taking off our shoes and feeling the ground beneath our feet, we can, symbolically, reconnect with creation—and our sense of our humanity, our createdness.

Another way of celebrating identity and wholeness is to encourage your congregation to feel their pulses. Once, we mixed a sample of a heartbeat with some evocative music, and asked everyone to feel their hearts beating at the same time. In this, we could celebrate the life-force that flows through us; we could remember our physicality, and help reconnect our bodies with our spirits. We then asked people to put their thumb prints on to a sheet of paper. This helped to celebrate our own individuality— not one print is the same as another—and yet our connectedness —we are not the same, yet we dwell together. We are whole individuals, yet we comprise a greater whole. These examples are so simple they are laughable; yet by stopping to take your pulse, you also take the pulse of your spirituality, your wholeness, your well-being. It's worth a try.

What is it about sitting on a surfboard beyond the breaking waves on a beautiful, clear morning that is so wonderful? It is the smell and taste of the salty sea, the sound of the pounding waves, the cry of the seagulls, the spray on your face, the cool, silky water, the warm glow of the sun, the anticipation and excitement of the next wave on the horizon, the good feeling in your body from the endorphins released by the last ride, the camaraderie of fellow surfers out there with you... It is about an entire sensory experience. It is the engagement of the full range of senses. And so it should be with our worship.

When we are worshipping God we should do so with our whole being. That means becoming more authentically human; it means drawing out our true identities and being free to be ourselves before God and each other; it means accepting the outsider, and incorporating their culture within our worship; it means celebrating all facets of our humanity, and using the full range of creativity which God has placed within us. We want to feel a sense of excitement and anticipation, awe or even trepidation, as we worship. Such are the things that make us feel alive—fully human—and that is how we should feel as we approach the living God with our true selves.

NINE

Dreaming on

Throughout this book we've stressed the need to nurture a positive attitude towards creativity. And while we have given you some 'alternative' examples, if you carry one thing away from this it should be that it's possible for you and your congregation or worship group to revitalize your own worship in your own way. While the 'ready to use' resources of the Christian subculture have had many positive effects, they have also made people quite lazy (or lacking in confidence) when it comes to mining the huge potential for creativity that even the smallest groups have.

There have been significant cultural changes in recent years, and alternative worship groups have been at the forefront of developing a response to these. If we are to take this kind of change seriously, perhaps we can start by understanding that the way we 'do' church should never be set in concrete and allowed to stand for a hundred years. The way we 'do' church can (and probably should) flow with different cultures—so long as the emphasis always remains on how to 'be' church: that is, that the end goal itself should be to create a genuine community of believers, not a flashy series of services.

But in all this, the role of the worship leader may need to be redefined. If that's you, be prepared to at least be flexible; at best, the role may evolve into something quite radically different from the norm—a role that suits your local church within your local community. Rather than seeing yourself as the all-singing, all-dancing front-person, you might instead focus on your role as facilitator, enabling the people within your congregation to creatively engage in and express worship to their Creator.

It is sad to say that for the best of reasons (a sense of responsibility and leadership) or the worst (the proud sense that 'only I can do it'), our worship often ends up being a one-man or one-woman show. Jesus made it clear that Christian service is no place for inflated egos or self-promotion. In Matthew 22:37–39 he commands us to 'love the Lord your God with all your heart, and with all your soul and with all your mind' and to 'love your neighbour as yourself'. If we are genuinely to love others, we also need to know what it is to love ourselves—with a *healthy* self-respect that means we no longer strive for kudos. When it is centred on the reality of genuine community and focused on the divine, creative worship can truly flow, as people move from being passive receivers to active and valued contributors.

The new breed of worship leader will need to develop their own skills in understanding and encouraging others. You might need to nudge people out of their 'comfort zones'—the safe places where they have settled. Using the journey metaphor again, we should be moving onwards, as travellers journeying towards the promised land. To journey is at times a struggle; we expose ourselves to new and unusual experiences and cultures, and we find out things about ourselves that perhaps we'd never have known if we'd stayed at home.

As you begin to create, this raises more and more issues. You will need to balance honesty with encouragement and nurture; and such honesty can only take place in the context of community. 'Doing' church and 'being' church therefore become inextricably connected. For example, how do you handle the situation when a well-meaning member of the congregation wants to lead some singing but is tone deaf? The way in which the dynamics and conflicts within your group are handled—and there will always be disputes!—is absolutely crucial in creating and maintaining an active, dynamic and creative community of worshippers. Some worship groups such as *Warehouse* in York have even brought in people experienced in leading group work to explore issues of group dynamics.

At *Live On Planet Earth* we would go on retreats, to share a meal and some worship, and to explore the issues relating not only to the service and the needs of those outside the group, but also those arising from within. So often with churches—especially those engaged in new or pioneering work—there is such a focus on mission that the needs of those at the heart of the community become neglected. Certainly, a balance needs to be struck, but the temptation is to want to change the world when you haven't yet changed yourselves. Remember: small is beautiful, and the future is local.

We have also said that your acts of worship should be 'owned' by you and your community. Ian Mobsby, from the *Epicentre* arts and creative worship group in Battersea, has said that one of the key ideas he has taken from his involvement in a number of alternative groups is of 'an integrated view of church and culture with music and creative expression that is resonant with that of the *local* culture'.

As you begin to integrate a greater variety of gifts and abilities within your worship, remember to value the *process* of creating services. What about the people who are involved in painting backdrops, taking photos for slides, preparing video loops and all the other behind-the-scenes activities? How can you make sure they feel that they are contributing to the worship experience, and that what they are doing is *in itself* worship?

While the process of creativity is not a science (and would probably suffer from an inflexible approach or attitude), it is well worth developing a framework within which creativity can develop —especially if you are to keep a stream of creative ideas flowing over a long period. You can't get around the fact that it takes a lot of collective energy and effort to be creative. The reality is that for many groups, especially those without a committed and enthusiastic team, the effort falls on one or two people, which becomes too much to bear. All too often, creative people on the fringes have had negative experiences of church and its leaders (especially when they perceive that their creativity has been stifled, ignored or rejected). They may need particular encouragement to participate fully. Before you start, you need to set in place a sustainable support network. Too often we expect creativity to emerge mysteriously from the ether. The reality is that for most of us, a little structure can go a long way to providing a clean, fresh canvas upon which to paint.

Teamwork

All too often, when people are asked to contribute to a service, it comes as a token act of condescension from a worship leader: 'Would you mind doing this reading for me for Sunday morning's service?' This is not empowering! The experience can often end up being unsatisfactory (if they have no control over the passage, for example, or when it is being read). The sociologist John Lofland, in his research into the 1980s peace movement in the United States, tried to determine how the groups managed to maintain such ongoing fervent and costly involvement. His conclusion was that 'soaring interest' which resulted in 'intensive interaction' was represented by and resulted in 'the pinnacle of integration'.[25] The more people are interested and have an opportunity to get involved, the more comprehensively they will be integrated within the group or community, which in turn results in more interaction and greater involvement. These things feed into and thrive from one another. Conversely, someone who has little opportunity to get involved in their community will soon feel left out and lose interest. It is important to remember that we are not trying to keep people happy so that our church stays big: we are hoping to create a thriving community of creative and authentic followers of Jesus.

If we want creative services, we need to get others involved as early as possible in the process, giving them a good say in what is going to happen, and not holding on to the reins of power too tightly. As you give power away, the community grows in interest and confidence, and it grows together. To put it simply, people are turned off by authoritarian institutions and hierarchies (and their trappings), but they can be encouraged and inspired by involvement in grassroots activities in which they feel a genuine part.

Such a sense of belonging might legitimately precede a conversion experience. It may seem strange to many evangelicals, but the act of participating in creating worship may be a prompt and an encouragement to those at the beginning of their 'faith journey'. This was certainly our experience with many young people at *Live On Planet Earth* and if it works with young people there is no reason why it shouldn't work with others—with the artists, the dancers, the musicians and all the other creative people in your locality.

You might begin to see how a variety of elements we have mentioned in this book come together here: the theological perspectives of faith as a journey, the embrace of our innate God-given creativity and an attitude of inclusiveness and dialogue rather than separatism and duality. All these things serve to create a rather different model of church from that with which we, along with many of our contemporaries, were brought up—and one that not only 'works' but is thoroughly liberating and exhilarating.

Practical steps

So, typically, you may have got a little group of people from your church together to explore the possibility of starting something 'alternative' or 'creative'. Probably the first thing you would need to decide is whether you are going to try to come up with some ideas to integrate into an existing service or whether you want to set up something in addition to what your existing church provides. You might want to spend some time developing and trying out ideas within the 'safe' environment of your group, allowing for organic growth as people make a positive choice to join in with what you are doing. It is important to set up some ground rules in terms of how you make decisions, what you expect from each other in terms of commitment and support, the parameters or boundaries of the group and so on. However unimportant this may seem, it is vital to ensure that people's expectations are properly voiced right from the start.

As you begin the process, beware not to overstretch yourselves. Remember, in the excitement of new beginnings, not to neglect the need to be realistic. You will not know how much effort is required to facilitate a creative worship experience for a large congregation until you have finished the first service. So, if this is what you want to do, try a one-off and then evaluate how often the group could commit to such an undertaking.

Service rotation

Some groups, especially those meeting on a weekly basis, set up repeatable services that incorporate elements of continuity which can be creatively added to. *Warehouse* includes a labyrinth service and *Grace* a regular Eucharist service. As time goes on, you may find this a helpful way of creating a maintainable rhythm— remembering of course that things can and probably should be changed from time to time.

Themes

Once you have decided the format for your creative worship, it would be well worth doing some research on issues affecting your local community. Why not ask people what issues concern them? It is important to try to be flexible and responsive to the concerns of the community. Don't plan everything so much that you can't respond to what is happening. At *Live On Planet Earth*, when a number of our group were leaving to go to college and university, we held a service which examined the themes of 'home', 'desert', 'exile' and 'promised land'—to facilitate a healthy process of saying goodbye and moving on. The story of the Israelites struck a chord with many of them. The Bible came alive in a new way as they saw connections with their own lives.

Why not arrange a survey of those in your worship community, or even within the wider local community? You might be surprised at the answers—and you will find a range of themes and issues that you can then set about exploring in the light of the Bible.

Creatively, it is worth giving people time to go away and think. Remember, the creative process is not automatic, but takes time and work. If you are planning a series in advance, an extra two months' worth of preparation is likely to yield much more stimulating responses than a hastily thrown-together service. You will probably have someone who is very keen on listening to music (though they may not be a gifted musician) and who has a wonderful CD collection. Ask them to think about some tunes that could fit in with the forthcoming themes. Do the same with poetry, art, drama and the like.

Planning and evaluation meetings

At *LOPE* we found at least one scheduled planning meeting a month was vital in order to nurture our creativity. We would spend time assessing the previous meeting and looking at areas on which we could improve. The idea is not to put on a highly polished production, although a balance needs to be struck between this and a slack attitude that leads to embarrassing pauses while someone turns on the microphone or rewinds a video. Things that can be improved upon and allow for a better 'flow' should be addressed in a supportive and loving way.

Failure

That said, it is vital that if we want to encourage creativity we must not be scared of trying things that fail. Failure is not a problem. We believe that the fear of failure and a lack of tolerance of things that don't work have led to a distinct curbing of creativity within the church. This is probably best explained by another example. When we first decided to have a go at doing a Labyrinth service at *LOPE*, the idea was explained to the whole team and some people expressed the valid opinion that some of our young people might feel too intimidated by the whole experience. It was tempting to worry that no one would bother coming. This was accentuated by the difficulty of explaining what it might even look like. Those of us who had come up with the idea didn't really know either—we knew that it was something that would have to 'come together' on the day. Yet we decided to take the risk, and to support one another in doing so. We had tried unusual things in the past and they had worked, so the decision was made to go ahead.

As it turned out, the service worked well and people across the generations participated in it together. There was no embarrassment. But the real test would have been had it totally fallen flat. It is in situations like this where the attitude of the team and group is vital if an ongoing creativity is to be nurtured and promoted. You could even go so far as to say that unless you are trying ideas that *do* fail from time to time, you aren't really pushing the boundaries of creativity at all. You are remaining within your comfort zones.

Brainstorming

Sit down together as a group and bat ideas around (having given the theme some constructive thought before the meeting). This can be a time when people really put their credibility within the group on the line. It is important to permit the discussion of ideas without anyone being put down or denigrated. Sometimes the weirdest ideas can become the most wonderful if you run with them and allow others to come in with a new and creative angle on them. Think back to some of the symbolic acts we described in Chapter 7. Some of these would never have happened had the climate not been one of positive encouragement.

Alternative worship can be dazzlingly technological or wonderfully simple. Those who have already blazed the trail would say one thing: this is not a movement, and it is not a blueprint to be copied. The aim of this book, as with the aim of anything 'alternative' in worship, is to help unlock creativity within local people at a local level. What may work in Cranbrook may well not work in Clapham, and vice versa.

You need not be controversial nor start a revolution nor leave your church to participate in alternative methods of worship. For some, it may mean draping banners, connecting TV sets, getting the video projector going and bringing in some rave DJs. For others, it may mean breaking for a few seconds of silence in a housegroup meeting, while you light a candle to consider why Jesus really is the 'light of the world'.

As we asked earlier, one of the questions on our minds as we seek to be effective Christians in today's world should be, 'In an image-saturated culture, what does it mean to be made in the image of God?' That is a question that could spark, in itself, an entire series of alternative worship services! But it is also a question that should make us think about how we reflect and represent God as the Church here on earth. The first thing we read that God does in the Bible is create. In the beginning, God created.

Look around you. Wonder at the beauty and complexity of creation. Look at the horizon that stretches before you and feel the awe of distance and magnitude. Look down at your feet, at the seeds of a dandelion, or the legs of a bee, or even the weeds growing through a crack in the pavement, and marvel. You don't have to go far to realize that creativity is wrapped up in God's being, and our being. We were made to worship. We were made to be creative. We were made to be whole. We can but dream.

The end of one journey means the start of another. We started this book with a section from the inward journey of the Labyrinth. We would like to end with the outward one. We hope that it all makes some sense, because we believe that a divine spark can be fanned into flame. You can make a difference.

As we have met with God, and received from him, think about taking the light out into the world. And about what it might illuminate.

Even if you are only a bright spark, kindle.
Kindle the life and the light you received from the heart of the Son.
You might get fired up.
You might blaze a trail,
stand up for others,
seek out injustice,
protest on behalf of the innocent,
carry a torch for the unloved,
demonstrate for love.
Demonstrate love itself.

Mary was also given a challenge. She was asked to carry The Word, the pulse of the cosmos within her.
She literally carried God into the world.

Mary said yes and changed the course of history—
took a gamble on the divine,
flouted the odds,
evened the score with darkness,
carried the light of the world and allowed it to shine.
So that we might see it, and respond.

She had a choice, as we have a choice.
Choice cuts:
sometimes like a sword to the heart.
It did for her.

Choose carefully.
Jesus was no robot—
he made agonizing choices.
Stood up, stood out
and was crucified for it.
Look where that got him, they said.
It got him all the way to us.

You can choose a lifestyle.
Or you can choose life.
The choice, as they say, is yours.

So where do we go from here? As the journey seems to be ending, it is
only just beginning.
We are caught between a world that is passing, and a world that is yet
to come. A world of the now, and the not yet...

Someone once spoke of a road less travelled.
Of a narrow path.

Today, we are going on a journey.[26]

1   'Ambient' is a loose term which describes any music that creates a relaxing atmosphere. More specifically, it refers to a genre of electronic 'dance' music that is typically used in 'chill-out' rooms in nightclubs where clubbers go to relax, away from the dance rooms. A good example of this is found on the *Freezone* CDs referred to in the Appendix of Resources.

2   'Recontextualize' means to work out what our worship might look like in our context or life-situations. Essentially it means applying the culture to the practices of worship and vice versa.

3   For a comprehensive account, see Roland Howard's *The Rise and Fall of the Nine O'Clock Service: A Cult within a Church* (Mowbray, 1996).

4   Peter Brierley, *The Tide is Running Out* (Christian Research, 2000), p. 67.

5   Malcom Hamilton, *The Sociology of Religion* (Routledge, 1995), p. 177.

6   Andrew Walker, *Telling the Story* (SPCK, 1996), p. 190.

7   Colin Gunton, *The One, the Three and the Many: God, Creation and the Culture of Modernity* (Cambridge University Press, 1993).

8   Malcom Hamilton, op. cit., p. 172.

9   From an unpublished paper by Graham Cray entitled 'From Here to Where?—The Culture of the Nineties', and cited by Dave Tomlinson in *The Post-Evangelical* (Triangle, 1995), p. 75.

10   Fritjof Capra, David Steindl-Rast and Thomas Matus, *Belonging to the Universe: Explorations on the Frontiers of Science and Spirituality* (Harper, SanFrancisco, 1992).

11   Neil MacGregor, 'An Advocate for Art', *Third Way*, March 2000, p. 18.

12   The issue of copyright is a somewhat grey area. We approached a number of film producers and TV companies when we started *LOPE*, asking for permission to use film clips for loops or in their own right. The typical response was that if we were using occasional short clips of films in a non-profit-making context such as a church service, they had no problem with us using it and there would be no charge. If you were charging people to come in, there would be a difference, we assume. In addition, many of the resources produced by alternative and creative worship groups are designed and sold to be used in a worship context and come with permission included.

     However, the point which we continue to emphasize is that, wherever possible, you should use your own material even if it is of an inferior quality, because this is all about being creative. Sometimes you can draw inspiration from others but we want you to break out of the culture which dictates that you are dependent on someone else for creative input. To paraphrase that proverb: give someone a resource book and they will have a term's worth of ideas; teach them the ability to think creatively and they will have access to a lifetime's worth of creative ideas.

13 James MacMillan, 'Sound of Heart', *Third Way*, June 1999, p. 19.

14 Ibid.

15 Douglas Coupland, *Life after God* (Simon & Schuster, 1995)

16 Simon Jenkins, *Windows into Heaven* (Lion, 1998).

17 The Eucharist is clearly a central element of Christian worship. For many alternative worship groups, imagining ways in which we can reconnect it to our lives is vital. *Grace* have devoted much time and effort in this area, experimenting with different eucharistic prayers and liturgies as well as exploring the myriad concepts it provokes when the Eucharist is allowed to connect with contemporary culture. In many ways, this culminated in the Sunday morning Eucharist service at Greenbelt in 1999. The book *Mass Culture* (ed. Pete Ward, BRF, 1999) gives a more detailed explanation of this and includes a chapter by Jonny Baker regarding the work done by *Grace* in recontextualizing the Eucharist.

18 Colin E. Gunton, *The Actuality of Atonement: A Study of Metaphor, Rationality and the Christian Tradition* (T. & T. Clark, 1988), pp. 29ff.

19 Dave Tomlinson, *The Post-Evangelical* (Triangle, 1995), pp. 93ff.

20 Taken from Jonny Baker's MA thesis on alternative worship and contemporary culture, which quotes Mike Riddell et al., *The Prodigal Project: Journey into the Emerging Church* (SPCK, 2000), p. 75.

21 'Cyber-feminism' is the amalgamation of an inclusivist, pro-feminist theology with the world of cyber culture—that is, a culture where most communication, interaction and relationships are electronically mediated.

22 Marshall Pickering, 1995.

23 As quoted in 'Our Irrelevant Church' by Madeleine Bunting in *The Guardian*, 20 March 1998.

24 *Grace* fanzine, December 1998.

25 John Lofland, 'The Soaring of Social Movements: American Peace Activism, 1981–1983' at www.data.fas.harvard.edu/cfia/priscs/s92lofla.htm.

26 By Brian Draper, Kevin Draper and Ana Draper.

Books

Peter Brierley, *The Tide is Running Out*, Christian Research, 2000.

Fritjof Capra, David Steindl-Rast and Thomas Matus, *Belonging to the Universe: Explorations on the Frontiers of Science and Spirituality*, Harper, San Francisco, 1992.

Douglas Coupland, *Life After God*, Simon and Schuster, 1994.

Douglas Coupland, *Polaroids from the Dead*, Flamingo, 1996.

Douglas Coupland, *Generation X: Tales for an Accelerated Culture*, Abacus, 1991.

Graham Cray et al., *The Post-evangelical Debate*, SPCK, 1997.

John Drane, *Evangelism for a New Age: Creating Churches for the Next Century*, Marshall Pickering, 1994.

William Gibson, *Neuromancer*, Harper Collins, 1984.

Colin E. Gunton and Daniel Hardy (ed.), *On Being the Church: Essays on the Christian Community*, T & T Clark, 1989.

Colin Gunton, *The One, the Three and the Many: God, Creation and the Culture of Modernity*, Cambridge University Press, 1993.

Colin Gunton, *The Actuality of Atonement: A Study of Metaphor, Rationality and the Christian Tradition*, T & T Clark, 1988.

David Harvey, *The Condition of Postmodernity*, Blackwell, 1990.

John Henstridge, *Step Into the Light*, BRF, 2000.

David Hilborn, *Picking up the Pieces: Can Evangelicals Adapt to Contemporary Culture?*, Hodder and Stoughton, 1997.

Roland Howard, *The Rise and Fall of the Nine O'Clock Service: A Cult within the Church*, Mowbray, 1996

Simon Jenkins, *Windows into Heaven*, Lion, 1998.

David Lyon, *Jesus in Disneyland: Religion in Postmodern Times*, Polity Press, 2000.

J.R. Middleton and B.J. Walsh, *Truth is Stranger than It Used to Be*, SPCK, 1995.

M. Scott Peck, *The Road Less Travelled: A New Psychology of Love*, Arrow Books, 1978.

Mike Riddell, Mark Pierson and Cathy Kirkpatrick, *The Prodigal Project*, SPCK, 2000.

Mike Riddell, *Godzone: A Guide to the Travels of the Soul*, Lion, 1992.

Mike Riddell, *altspirit@metro.m3: Alternative Spirituality for the Third Millennium*, Lion, 1997.

Paul Roberts, *Alternative Worship and the Church of England*, Grove Books Ltd, 1999.

Dave Tomlinson, *The Post-evangelical*, Triangle, 1995.

Andrew Walker, *Telling the Story*, SPCK, 1996.

Sue Wallace, *Multisensory Prayer*, Scripture Union, 2000.

Pete Ward (ed), *Mass Culture: Eucharist and Mission in a Post-modern World*, BRF, 1999.

David Wells, *No Place for Truth*, IVP, 1993.

Websites

www.greenbelt.org.uk.altgrps.html—this site has details of many of the alternative worship groups based in the UK and worldwide and includes links to their websites.

www.labyrinth.org.uk—for details of the labyrinth.

www.trinity-bris.ac.uk/altw_faq—a list of resources and 'frequently asked questions' about alternative worship.

www.geocities.com/SoHo/Lofts/9367/—The Ship of Fools.

www.holyspace.org/welcome.html—Holy Space—online worship, links and resources.

http://freespace.virgin.net/adam.baxter/grace/fresh.html—for full details of the *Grace* service based in Ealing—videos and music available.

www.embody.co.uk—an interactive online worship experience.

www.thirdway.org.uk/

www.iona.org.uk.wgp/catalog.htm

alt.worship@niweb.com—an internet discussion forum.

www.vurch.com

Music

Grace have produced some CDs which can be used in worship—more details at http://freespace.virgin.net/adam.baxter/grace/fresh.html or grace.london@btinternet.com or from Proost, http://www.proost.co.uk/ or from 38 Airedale Road, Ealing, London, W5 4SD.

Late Late Service—music from the *LLS* can be accessed via the Greenbelt website (see above).

Visions—for music from the *Visions* service based in York, go to www.abbess.demon.co.uk/visions.

The ambient *Freezone* compilation series can provide inspiration: *Freezone* is produced on the SSR label.

Videos

One Small Barking Dog have produced a number of excellent videos of visuals which provoke thought or help to create a worshipful atmosphere, they include permission for use in worship.

www.osbd.org/index.html

www.trinity-bris.ac.uk/altw_faq—for suggestions on videos which can be used in worship.